DOWN MANY A ROAD

The Story of Shell in Ireland
1902-2002

By

Bob Montgomery

Dreoilín

Almost 5,000 Irish men and women
have served Shell in Ireland.
This book is dedicated to them.

Other books by the same author:
An Irish Roadside Camera 1896-1906
The 1903 Irish Gordon Bennett Race

Dreoilín Album Series:
Early Motoring in Ireland
Leslie Porter – Ireland's Pioneer Racing Driver
The Irish International Grand Prix 1929-1931
The Phoenix Park Speed Trials 1903
The Irish Gordon Bennett Race 1903
Ford Manufacture and Assembly at Cork 1919-1984

Published by Dreoilín Specialist Publications Limited,
Tankardstown, Garristown, County Meath, Ireland.
Trade enquiries to Dreoilín Publications Limited.
Telephone (+353 1) 8354481

First published in 2002

Copyright © 2002 Bob Montgomery

ISBN 1-902773-11-X
A CIP record for this title is available from the British Library

Design by Dreoilín Specialist Publications Limited.
Typeset in 10/13 Stone Serif by Computertype Limited, and printed in the Republic of Ireland
by ColourBooks Ltd., Unit 105, Baldoyle Industrial Estate, Baldoyle, Dublin 13.

Contents

Foreword

One of the most pleasant responsibilities I inherited on becoming Managing Director & Chairman of Irish Shell in 1996 was to attend the round of Retired Staff Christmas parties. Apart from the culinary burden of facing turkey and ham for dinner on five consecutive days, it gave me a wonderful opportunity to meet many of the people who had been key participants in Irish Shell over many years.

So I sat, I ate, I said the few 'boss-man' words – and then I started to listen. I heard so many wonderful stories about Shell *"in the good old days"* from people who had worked in many different parts of the operation – from management and staff, from drivers, operatives, clerical and sales staff – from all parts of the country. All of them were certain in their belief that they had contributed to creating an Irish Shell that had played a central role in Irish life and of which they could be proud.

After a couple of years of this annual pilgrimage it struck me that what I was hearing was not just the story of Irish Shell, but was actually a reflection of Irish society as it changed and developed over the 20th century. The business of Irish Shell responded to the growing new Irish economy, as the horse was replaced by the tanker, and petrol became more important than lamp oil.

That was the genesis of this history. This is not the story of the corporate Irish Shell. Rather it is a record of the social and economic times of Ireland as reflected in the chronicles of an oil company and its people.

Michael Forde
Chairman
Irish Shell Limited
1996-2001

Author's Introduction

Researching and writing this history of Shell operations in Ireland has been a particular pleasure for me. Right from the inception of the project, Michael Forde – from whom came the original idea for this volume – made it clear that he envisaged a book that focused on the social history of Ireland, as experienced through the story of Irish Shell and its people adapting and changing as the social and economic environment around it changed.

At first, with but a few notable exceptions, it seemed that people's memories of their days in Shell might be few and far between, and I fell back on that wonderful resource, The Guinness Segrave Library of the Royal Irish Automobile Club Archive in Dawson Street, Dublin. There, my search, most particularly through the pages of R J Mecredy's *Motor News* magazine, was amply rewarded as I discovered a rich stream of Shell history recorded in its pages. Many valuable insights into the early days of Shell in Ireland flowed from its pages and in particular, light was thrown upon the earliest days of the company and the men and women who were its lifeforce.

By the time this material had been yielded up, the flow of reminiscences and memories from past and serving Shell people had begun to flow in earnest. And what a rich flow of material it turned out to be! Booklets, letters, personal reminiscences and most valuable of all, photographs, kept down the years, were generously offered. Most of the principal sources of this material are listed at the beginning of this book but there were many more who supplied material, even humble snapshots taken with a simple box camera, which today are the only record of some half-remembered event of long ago. Should I have neglected to acknowledge any individual source of this material, I beg your forgiveness. The response from all concerned was tremendous and made my role particularly interesting.

It is my belief that we each live two lives – our own and that of the times in which we live – and of course, a company like Shell is no different. Therefore, I have tried to include many items, photographs, publications and other memorabilia as touchstones of their time, hoping that they will awaken for the reader other memories of Shell. I hope that you will find my endeavours worthwhile and that I have done justice to the men and women who together have constituted Irish Shell down through its rich and varied history.

Bob Montgomery,
Spring 2002

Acknowledgements

An enormous number of people helped in the preparation of this book, either by generously lending valuable photographs and other long-cherished memories of their time with Shell, or by allowing me to record their memories of the company and their colleagues. So many different people helped in so many differing ways that it would be impossible to record all of them here, however, the assistance of the following, many of whom lent photographs as well as giving me their personal recollections, was particularly appreciated: Harry Jordan, Cecil Gilliard and the late Joe Coffey, Stanley G S Russell, John Lally, Arthur Henderson, Jim Birmingham, Basil Carr, Paddy Maher, Claire Dumbleton, May Murphy, Alfie Duff, Carmel Mallaghan, Nicholas Nolan, Frank Blennerhassett, John 'Sean' McMahon, Deirdre Byers, the late Jim Kennedy, Derek McMahon, Sean and Seamus Kelly, Noel O'Reilly, the late Dan Daly, Pat Halpin, Gerry O'Neill, Aidan O'Carroll, Jim Beveridge, John Withrington, Paddy Prendergast, Vincent Sheridan, Cormac McGuinness, Larry Hughes, Paddy Foley, 'Bill' Moore, Oliver Talbot, Des Ryan, P J Quinlivan, Chris Hosford, Tony O'Loughlin, T G 'Gerry' O'Neill, Paddy Dunne, Joan Curran, Gordon Johnston, the late Paddy Glynn, John Buggle, Ned Sweeney, Gerry McManus, Noel Harris and Patrick Lynch.

Others who helped especially were Joanne McWilliam, Shell International, Meena Patel, Curator, Shell Art Collection at Beaulieu, Steve Latham, British National Motor Museum, Beaulieu, Angela Brady of Shell *Live*WIRE, The Society of the Irish Motor Industry, Shell-Mex BP Archive at the University of Warwick, The National Library of Ireland and The Royal Irish Automobile Club Archive.

A special word of thanks is due to Ann Doherty (granddaughter of Hugh St G Harpur), Mary McCarthy (widow of Noel Nunan), John Finnucane, artist Vincent Killowry, An Post, Alec Bell, Des Murphy, Noel Tierney, Declan Fallon, Zoë Devlin and Annette Martin. Gerry Gilmore and Jack Dunne provided help in so many ways that this book would have been impossible without their valued input, and finally, Michael Forde, who had the idea for this book and who provided the opportunity for me to record this significant piece of Irish social and industrial history before it was lost forever through the passage of time.

Bob Montgomery

A Chronology of Shell Operations in Ireland

1902	Distribution depots are established at various strategic rail locations around the country.
1903/4	The first bulk storage installation in Ireland established jointly by the Consolidated Petroleum Company and Shell at Foynes.
1904	'Shell' Motor Spirit becomes available throughout the United Kingdom, including Ireland.
1905	September – The General Petroleum Company opens offices at No. 8 Bachelor's Walk, Dublin, for the sale of Shell Motor Spirit and other petroleum products - the company already have a store at No. 11 Upper Mayor Street, North Wall, where a stock of Shell Motor Spirit is kept. The manager of the office at Bachelor's Walk is Mr A P Coppinger.
1906	April – The earliest advertisement for 'Shell' to be placed in an Irish publication appears in the *Motor News*.
1907	The British Petroleum Company takes over distribution and sale of Shell products in the United Kingdom.
1908	The British Petroleum Company Limited exhibits at the January 1908 Irish Motor Show. Mr Hutchinson, *"the firm's Dublin representative"* is in charge of the stand.
1908	December 22nd – The Asiatic Petroleum Company takes a lease on several acres of land at Alexandra Road, Dublin, and signs an agreement with Dublin Port & Docks Board for the laying of railway lines between its depot and North Wall Point.
1912	Shell supplies fuel for the Dublin to Belfast Air Race.
1916	January – J A Burns is appointed as the company's first Irish Manager.
1916	December 31st – The end of Agreement with the British Petroleum Company to distribute and market Shell products in Ireland.
1917	January 1st – Shell Marketing Company Limited takes over sales and distribution of Shell products in Ireland from British Petroleum Company Limited.
1917	First Shell office established at No. 70 Grafton Street, Dublin.
1919	Alcock and Brown make the first non-stop crossing of the Atlantic by aeroplane. Fuelled by Shell, their epic flight ends in a Connemara bog.
1919	'Permit' strike brings motor traffic to a virtual standstill.
1920	Military authorities take control of the Shell depots and lorries.
	Shell holds its first annual dinner dance.
1921	Shell markets a range of lubricating oils for the first time in Ireland.
1922	Upon the foundation of the Irish Free State, Shell-Mex (Dublin) Limited takes over the Shell and Eagle Oil business in Southern Ireland.
1926	McMullan Brothers draw supplies from Irish Shell, beginning an association which continues to this day.

1928   The first successful East to West crossing of the Atlantic achieved by the *Bremen*. Shell-Mex (Dublin) supplies the lubricants.

1929-31 Shell-Mex (Dublin) supports the Irish Grand Prix series held in Dublin's Phoenix Park.

1930   Captain Hugh St. G Harpur becomes Managing Director of Shell-Mex (Dublin) Limited succeeding J A Burns.

December – Shell-Mex (Dublin) Limited move to new headquarters at No. 21 Dame Street, Dublin.

1931   December – Shell-Mex (Dublin) Limited and Irish BP Limited merge to become Shell and BP (Irish Free State) Limited.

1932   Shell Managing Director, Captain Hugh St. G Harpur, tours the company's depots by air.

A Shell base is established at Foynes for the re-fuelling of flying boats.

1933   Shell and BP (I.F.S.) Limited changes its name to Irish Shell Limited.

1935   Irish Shell and the Alliance and Dublin Consumers Gas Company jointly blend benzole and petrol to produce 'Irishell Benzole Mixture' as an alternative to petrol.

1936   Irish Shell services the refuelling needs of the pioneering flying-boats operating from Foynes.

1936-38 The Government introduces a requirement that the oil companies purchase industrial alcohol made from surplus potato production, for blending with motor spirit.

1939   October – Rationing introduced. Combined Delivery System agreed between Government and the oil companies. 'Pool Board' set up. Petrol sold on a 'no-brand' basis.

1944   Remaining petrol ration withdrawn

1948   Shell depot is established at Dublin Airport.

T A Crawford-Young succeeds Captain Hugh St. G Harpur as Managing Director of Irish Shell.

Branded products return.

1949   January – Combined Delivery System ends.

Shannon Airport depot established.

1951   The company moves its headquarters from Dame Street to 13-16 Fleet Street, Dublin.

1951   December – Petrol rationing ends.

1952   Irish Shell establishes at Dublin the first bulk bitumen plant in the world not attached to a refinery.

1953   Inishowen Oil Company and The Shield Oil Company established as Irish Shell's first Authorised Distributors.

1955   July/August – Drivers Strike at Dublin Terminal.

1956   A Hydrant Refuelling System is introduced at Shannon Airport by Irish Shell.

Suez Crisis.

1957   A new terminal is officially opened at Cork.

1961   September 1st – Irish Shell Limited changes its name to Irish Shell and BP Limited.

1961   New Limerick Depot opened.

1964   March 31st – Bernard A Nolan succeeds T A Crawford- Young as Managing Director of Irish Shell and BP Limited.

1966	'Make Money' Petrol Promotion.
	Munster Simms acquired by Irish Shell.
1968	Irish Shell employee, Noel Nunan, loses his life in the crash of an Aer Lingus Viscount while flying from Cork to London.
1970	The company moves its headquarters from Fleet Street to No. 20 Lr. Hatch Street, Dublin.
	New facility opened at Dublin Airport.
	New Galway terminal established.
1973/4	OPEC Oil Crisis.
1976	January 1st – De-merger of Irish Shell and BP. Shell business now handled by Irish Shell Limited.
1980	November – Tanker drivers' strike.
1981	February – Tanker Drivers' strike. Defence Forces operate tanker fleet during drivers' strike.
	August – Jim M Beveridge succeeds Bernard Nolan as Managing Director of Irish Shell Limited.
1982	Autumn – First issue of *Eólas* – the *"Newsletter for Shell staff in Ireland"*.
1983	The company returns to profit after two years of serious losses.
1984	Legendary Austrian racing driver, Niki Lauda, visits Dublin to launch Shell Sport '85.
1986	March – John Withrington succeeds Jim Beveridge as Managing Director of Irish Shell.
1989	Government introduces Price Controls.
	Formula Shell petrol withdrawn from the Irish market.
	Shell Unleaded becomes the first Unleaded petrol to go on sale in Ireland.
1990	May – Patrick Lynch succeeds John Withrington as Managing Director of Irish Shell.
1991	Irish Shell receives the prestigious ISO9002 Award.
	The company headquarters are moved from Hatch Street to Beech Hill Office Campus at Clonskeagh.
1992	The first of a chain of new convenience 'Select' stores located on Irish Shell retail sites is opened at Fairies Cross, Tralee.
1993	The new Shell terminal at Cork is officially re-opened.
	Shell Chemicals Ireland takes over responsibility for marketing group petrochemical products in Northern Ireland from Shell Chemicals UK.
1995	Brent Spar deep-sea disposal crisis.
1996	Shell House the scene of a sit-in amid widespread interest by the Irish public in the plight of the Ogoni People of Nigeria.
	October – Michael Forde succeeds Patrick Lynch as Managing Director of Irish Shell, and is also appointed Chairman.
1998	'Shell in the Island of Ireland' programme achieves integration of Shell operations in Ireland.
	Shell Pura ultra-clean petrol launched.
1999	Irish Shell web site established.
2001	November – John McDonagh succeeds Michael Forde as Country Chairman of Shell in Ireland.
2002	Shell celebrates its centenary in Ireland.

Chapter 1

1902-1919: Beginnings

Right from the first Shell advertisements in Ireland in 1906, Shell advertising was bold and distinctive.

1902-1919 Ford Model T launched – Irish Crown Jewels stolen – Cars taxed on hp ratings – King George V visits Dublin – Titanic sinks with great loss of life – Carson organises Ulster Covenant – 'The Great Lockout' – Outbreak of The Great War – Home Rule Act suspended – Easter Rising – Battle of the Somme – Armistice – Alcock and Brown make the first non-stop transatlantic flight by aeroplane – First Dáil meets in the Mansion House – War of Independence begins

The modern oil industry which was destined to become so much a part of all our daily lives, was born in 1859, when 'Colonel' Edwin Drake drilled the first successful oil well at Pennsylvania in the United States. In those early days, the main aim of refining oil was to produce kerosene for lamp oil. Gasoline – or petrol – that essential ingredient of modern life, was regarded as a waste product and was burned off. The new drilling techniques led to a 'black gold rush', especially in the United States of America, with many eager entrepreneurs hoping to make their fortunes overnight. Some, often against great odds, succeeded and new companies were founded at a phenomenal rate. In 1903, two of these successful companies – The Shell Transport and Trading Company and the

Royal Dutch Petroleum Company – established a new joint venture, the Asiatic Petroleum Company, to further their joint interests. The Royal Dutch Petroleum Company had been founded in 1890 to develop oil fields in the East Indies, while the Shell Transport and Trading Company was largely a trading venture established by Marcus Samuel in 1897 to handle the transportation of Russian kerosene in bulk from the Black Sea through the Suez Canal to the Far East. Although the two companies retained their separate and distinct entities, the 1903 agreement enabled them to pool their expertise in drilling and refining with their skills in transport and marketing to become the selling agent throughout the world for East Indies oil production.

The exact date on which Shell products first went on sale in Ireland is bound up in the history of some of the many companies which were part in its earliest days of what we now call Shell. One of these, The Consolidated Petroleum Company Limited, began operations here as early as February 1902, when its Minute Book recorded the establishment of a depot on a site belonging to the Great Northern Railway at Dublin. This depot would have been primarily for the distribution of lamp oil and kerosene. Evidently, business in Ireland was promising enough for Consolidated to sign further agreements with the Great Northern Railway and also with the Great Western Railway during 1902 for additional depots to be sited at Drogheda, Carrick-on-Shannon, Westport, Longford, Ballina, Claremorris and Galway. This expansion continued in the following year and depots were added at Cork, Charlestown, Kells, Dungannon, Carrickmacross and Maryboro (now Portlaoise). Many of these locations are still the sites of various Shell installations today.

It also seems likely that an ocean storage facility was established at Foynes in County Limerick, on land belonging to Lord Monteagle, as early as 1902, although the actual purchase of the site was not completed until 1905. The site was, however, certainly in use for several years by the time the legal requirements for its purchase had been completed and the Company Minute Book records the payment of £1,019 to the Great Southern & Western Railway upon completion of the laying down of railway sidings on the site early in 1904. An interesting aside on the times is the recording in these minute books of an application from the firm's Dublin manager, a Mr J M Hutchinson, for leave of absence to travel to the United States of America for a month, during which time he proposed to leave the business in the charge of his Chief Clerk, W H Power. The Secretary was instructed *"to write agreeing to his request on condition that he sign a document drafted by the*

Foynes – First in Ireland

This postcard shows the deep-sea bulk storage depot at Foynes, County Limerick, which was established around 1902. Foynes was to play a pioneering role in Shell operations in Ireland over the next fifty years. The postcard shows the jetty at top and below the depot with the cooperage on the right. The postcard – which could be used to order Lamp Oil – dates from 1905/6 at which time Shell products were distributed and marketed by the British Petroleum Company.

company's solicitors undertaking full liability for the conduct of the business by his representative during his absence."

On May 10th 1904, the two companies – The Shell Transport and Trading Company and the Royal Dutch Petroleum Company – jointly formed the General Petroleum Company to oversee the distribution and storage of Shell products in Europe. Based in London, the General Petroleum Company took over ownership of Shell tank farms throughout Europe. In the last week of September of the following year, 1905, the company opened an office at No. 8 Bachelor's Walk, Dublin, for the sale of Shell products – mostly lamp oil and the increasingly popular Shell Motor Spirit. The company is recorded as already having a store in Dublin prior to that date at No. 11 Upper Mayor Street, North Wall, *"where a stock of Shell Motor Spirit is kept"*. The new office was under the management of Mr A P Coppinger who let it be known that *"any enquiries with regard to agencies for Shell spirit should be addressed to him...and would receive prompt attention."*

A short diversion to record the rise of motor spirit as a product is not out of place at this point in our story. The early motorist faced considerable confusion with regard to the fuel and oil he should use in his automobile's motor. This confusion was not helped by the naming of the various motor spirit products available which fell into two main types. The first of these was a light benzine (or benzoline) which in Britain had first been produced by a London oil-refining company, Carless, Capel and Leonard in 1890. They named their new product 'petrol' borrowing from the French word *'pétrole'* which confusingly means kerosene or paraffin oil. Several years later, they developed a more volatile spirit which they named 'gasoline'. The principal alternative to petrol was a coal-tar derivative developed by the great English engineer, Lanchester, which he called 'benzole' or 'benzene'. Confused? Well, the fledgling motorist certainly was and the early history of motoring is littered with stories of automobile fuel tanks being filled with the wrong product. Similar confusion prevailed in relation to lubricating oil, most of which had been animal-fat based until the advent of the automobile. One such story was told by a Major Nugent. The Major had acquired his first car in 1902, a 4½ hp De Dion and during one of his first journeys on it, *"found that there was very little oil in the crank chamber, and that I had no spare charge. In the innocence of my heart I filled up with salad oil and started the engine. At once dense clouds of greasy, black and evil-smelling smoke rose from under the car. The faces of my friends, who had been grouped in an appreciative circle round the car, grew grave, and one by one they silently stole away to a discreet distance. Nothing, however, happened beyond an extremely bad*

Horse-Drawn Days

The early days of Shell in Ireland were the days of horse-drawn deliveries. The Shell wagon was a familiar sight in most areas and was particularly used for the delivery of kerosene, then used extensively for home lighting.

RDS Spring Show 1911

The earliest photograph of a Shell display in Ireland is of these Shell products being displayed on the stand of the British Petroleum Company at the 1911 Spring Show of the Royal Dublin Society at their Ballsbridge, Dublin, Showgrounds. The British Petroleum Company continued to be responsible for the marketing and distribution of Shell products throughout Britain and Ireland up until the end of 1916.

17

smell, and so I started on my return journey to Dublin." As has often been remarked, early motorists, it seems, were never found wanting in initiative, even if their mechanical knowledge often left something to be desired!

In time, although it was correctly the name of one particular company's product, 'petrol' became the common name for motor fuel, rival companies being careful to name their product 'motor spirit'. (Indeed, in 1902, R J Mecredy writing in the *Motor News* in a short article attempting to clear up the confusion regarding names concluded *"that 'petrol' will continue to be the popular name."*) But having established the correct product to use, where did the early motorist obtain supplies? Prior to 1904/5 when supplies became much more generally available, a motorist ordered supplies from a depot and these were usually sent to him by rail. The rail companies didn't like transporting small quantities of petrol and charged insurance as well as freight on consignments which could add as much as 6d to the cost of a gallon. Late in 1902, the rail companies also required the vendor to sign a consignment note, undertaking to pay compensation for any damage that might arise. The various petrol suppliers decided that they would not sign this note and this in turn led to the rapid establishment of a network of depots throughout the country, agreement having been reached with the rail companies for bulk delivery to these depots. Should a motorist run short on a journey, his best option was to seek the aid of the local chemist who could probably supply benzine in glass jars in sufficient quantity to get him home again.

A list of *"Firms stocking Petrol or Motor Spirit"* in the *Motor News* magazine of January 6th 1906 lists a total of 51 locations – mostly hotels and cycle agents – throughout the entire island where supplies might be obtained. These supplies of petrol would have been in two gallon cans and it is reasonable to suppose that a large proportion of them would have been in the familiar Shell red can which had gone on sale throughout the United Kingdom in 1904, supplied in the first instance from the General Petroleum Company store at North Wall, Dublin. A common concern of the motoring public at this time was with regard to the possible exhaustion of petrol supplies owing *"to the extraordinary rapid rate at which demand is increasing"* and during a visit to the company's Dublin offices, F P S Harris of the General Petroleum Company sought to allay such fears, pointing out that *"the consumption of motor spirit must grow to vast dimensions before it can seriously affect a tax on the resources of the oil fields."*

Shortly after this, the earliest advertisement for 'Shell' that the author has been able to locate in an Irish publication, appeared in the April 21st

1906 issue of the fortnightly Irish Motor magazine, *Motor News*. This quarter page advertisement claims "MORE MILES ON ONE CAN OF SHELL MOTOR SPIRIT THAN ON ANY OTHER" and carries the address of the General Petroleum Company of 19-21 Billiter Street, London. This first advertisement must have generated some business for the company as the same advertisement was repeated one month later in the issue of May 12th of the same publication

Subsequent advertising during 1907 addressed a serious problem which the company was experiencing. This was the refilling of Shell cans by unscrupulous dealers with other brands of spirit. The company – now established in Belfast as well as in Dublin – reacted by taking full page advertisements declaring:

FOR YOUR OWN PROTECTION
IT IS ABSOLUTELY IMPERATIVE TO EXAMINE
OR INSTRUCT YOUR CHAUFFEUR TO EXAMINE EVERY CAN
AND SEE THAT THE 'SHELL' SEAL IS INTACT.
YOU MAY HAVE TO INSIST, BUT IT'S WORTH IT!

Our story now skips forward several years to 1908 – a year of great turmoil in Ireland. Agrarian unrest was widespread across the Irish countryside and occupied greatly the thoughts of the Chief Secretary for Ireland, Mr Birrel. The most militant protests took place in the Irish Midlands where landless labourers aggressively sought the division of large under-utilised farms. Mr Birell, in response, earnestly urged Parliament to bring about a speedy settlement of the land question by acquiring land and redistributing it into small holdings.

And this was not the only contentious issue facing Parliament with regard to Ireland. High taxes and the spiralling cost of the Irish administration were such that the House of Commons was told that they were placing an undue burden on the people of Ireland. In addition, women protested in the streets and in the courts over sentencing of women under *"man made laws."* Crime increased significantly in all of the major cities, and the Irish Crown Jewels, stolen the previous year, had yet to be recovered. (In fact, they never were recovered and their theft remained a major embarrassment to the administration).

In general, then, 1908 was a bad year for Ireland and the Irish economy. Employment was hard to come by, and a total of 39,082 Irishmen and women emigrated to America and to Britain. The single bright spot was Belfast where the shipyards were enjoying a period of boom and rising employment. A Post Office clerk lucky enough to be in employment could expect to earn 16s. a week, an amount which would hardly leave enough to take him to the Theatre Royal in Dublin's Hawkin's Street, where 'The Battle of Waterloo' was enjoying a long run to the city's well-to-do middle classes.

At the highly successful Irish Automobile Club Motor Show held at the premises of the Royal Dublin Society at Ballsbridge during the second week of January 1908, the British Petroleum Company Limited displayed a full range of Shell products. This reflected the distribution arrangement which had come into existence throughout Britain and Ireland for 'Shell' products the previous year following the amalgamation of Shell Transport and Royal Dutch in January 1907. Shell's *retail* business in Ireland, however was overseen by the Shell Marketing Company Limited based at 39 and 41 Parker Street, Kingsway, London. The Dublin operation looked after the territory of Ireland and was one of eight divisional offices spread throughout Britain and Ireland. As the catalogue for the Motor Show recorded:

This company...will have a good show of their drums and cases in which they supply the spirit. An advertising novelty which they are introducing at the

Show is a series of about a dozen picture postcards illustrating the success of Shell spirit in various uses for motor car purposes. They will also be exhibiting a coloured representation of Mr Edge during the course of his twenty-four hours drive at Brooklands, his remarkable performance on that occasion being obtained when using Shell spirit.

The 'Mr Edge' referred to here, was, of course, the famous pioneer motorist whose remarkable victory in the 1902 Gordon Bennett motor race had ultimately resulted in the staging of the 1903 race in Ireland. It is generally regarded that this event, more than any other, made the Irish public 'car-conscious'.

The stand was manned by Mr McHutchinson, *"the firm's Dublin representative."*

The first regular Shell advertising commenced with the *Motor News* magazines Show preview edition of January 1908. The advertisement proclaims:

> SHELL MOTOR SPIRIT.
> IT'S PERFECT PURITY!
> THAT'S THE POINT!

and carries the address of The British Petroleum Company Limited of 22 Fenchurch Street, London E.C. Thereafter, further regular advertisements for Shell continued to appear throughout 1908.

At the end of this year during which Shell's presence in Ireland grew considerably, the Company made an important investment in its Irish market. This occurred on December 22nd 1908, when the Asiatic Petroleum Company signed a lease on several acres of land at Alexandra Road, Dublin, where today a part of Shell's Dublin Terminal still stands. In taking the lease, the Asiatic Petroleum Company sought to establish a storage and distribution depot for Shell Petroleum products which would allow for the planned future expansion of their business in Ireland. At the same time, it signed an agreement with Dublin Port & Docks Board for the laying of railway lines between its planned depot and the pivotal goods railway terminal at North Wall Point.

From its inception, Shell showed a keen interest in the development of aviation and this interest manifested itself in Ireland when the Dublin to Belfast Air Race was held in 1912. Aviation had begun in Ireland with the foundation of the Irish Aero Club by members of the Irish Automobile Club at their premises in Dawson Street, Dublin, in November 1909. Amongst those who were founder members were John Boyd Dunlop of pneumatic tyre fame and Harry Ferguson, who would become the first to fly in Ireland on the last day of that year and whose name would become forever linked with his famous tractors and farm equipment. A hugely successful Aviation meeting was held at Leopardstown the following August, promoted and organised by the new club and an even more ambitious event – an air race from Dublin to Belfast – was held in 1912. Shell supplied fuel to the aviators who were, not unnaturally, very particular about the quality of the fuel used in their flying machines. In the race, strong winds prevented the competitors reaching their destination, the Show Grounds at Balmoral, and prizes were awarded on the basis of distance flown. Many of the aviators were loud in their praise of Shell's involvement in the race and their comments were widely advertised.

Indeed, for many years, the top grade of Shell motor spirit was sold as 'Shell Aviation Spirit' in golden, rather than the more familiar red cans.

During its first decade in Ireland, Shell supplied the rapidly growing Irish Motor Industry which was then experiencing an unprecedented period of growth, as well as selling large quantities of paraffin for lighting and gas

Wings over Leopardstown

The first Aviation Meeting in Ireland was organised by the Irish Automobile Club at Leopardstown Racecourse on August 29th and 30th 1910. Shell fuel was supplied to the three aviators present who demonstrated their machines.

The Farman biplane of Cecil Grace airborne over Leopardstown. Grace's parents had emigrated from Ireland to America, before settling in Chile, where Cecil was born.

Grace's Farman biplane being manhandled into position for take-off.

J Armstrong Drexel in his Bleriot monoplane. Drexel made several flights taking passengers aloft on the first day of the Meeting.

making spirit for private gas plants and houses. While competitors were importing paraffin and spirits in barrels, Shell had helped establish the first bulk storage installation in the country at Foynes which was built by the Consolidated Petroleum Company. It supplied kerosene and 680 spirit – a gas-making spirit for private domestic plant. The Foynes bulk installation reduced costs enormously and improved efficiency, but not everybody was pleased. Two farmers who had a contract with the company insisted on Shell fulfilling their contract to the letter. As a result a cooper was employed at Foynes to make barrels exclusively for these customers. The farmers, in turn, would cut in half the barrels specially made for them and use them as feeding troughs for their livestock! Other customers were more obliging and continued taking delivery from the horse-drawn tankers which remained in contract use right up to the mid-1930s (and even as late as the 1950s in County Cork because of the many narrow streets and steep hills there).

In fact, the development of Shell's retail network in Ireland was closely tied to the horse and cart in these early days. The ability of a horse-drawn wagon to travel from a depot to a dealer and back in a day dictated its growth. Drivers based in Dublin, travelling as far as Dunlavin, for example, only 40 miles south, had no alternative but to stay overnight. As a result of these difficulties, many informal arrangements were entered into which helped circumvent these problems. Often these were to the consternation of those Shell employees who were based elsewhere and were unused to Irish ways. Famously, one such case arose with regard to the difficulties involved in supplying fuel to Aranmore Island, off the remote north-west Donegal coast. Anything up to 30 barrels would be left in the care of the Burtonport stationmaster until the island boat turned up to collect them. A Shell inspector happened upon this arrangement and was horrified that company property should be left in the hands of a non-company employee. *"Is the stationmaster under contract?"* the inspector asked. *"Not at all,"* replied the delivery driver, *"He just does it to oblige me."*

Another interesting aspect of the business at this time was the differing price of petrol throughout the country, which proved an unfathomable mystery to some. A correspondent, writing in the *Motor News* in October 1914, reported:

> *Recently in Birr, I was charged 1s 10d per gallon for second grade spirit – a price at which I did not quibble. Galway's price was 1s 8d per gallon – reasonable enough in view of the fact that we pay 1s 7d in Dublin. But it was in the wilds of Connemara that prices varied in a strange fashion, not to be*

The Father of Irish Motoring

R J Mecredy – invariably 'Arjay' – is rightly titled the father of Irish motoring. His magazine, the Motor News, *was founded in 1900 when there were probably no more than 50 motorcars in Ireland. Involved in every aspect of the development of Irish motoring, Arjay encouraged companies such as Shell to become involved in the Irish market, reporting their activities with an accuracy rarely shown in the printed word through the pages of the* Motor News. *In the main photo, Arjay is shown in conversation with another great pioneer, John Boyd Dunlop, whose development of the pneumatic tyre profoundly affected the development of motoring.*

understood by any normal individual. For instance, at Cashel Hotel the price was 1s 9d per gallon, and this was the price I also paid at McKeown's Hotel at Leenane. As both these places are remote, and if spirit is got by rail it has to be carried a considerable distance, the price is not to be grumbled at. But at another hotel in the same district, situated close to the railway, the price is 2s per gallon. Furthermore, I found on enquiry that both first and second grade spirit are sold at the same price – surely a ridiculous arrangement, which may soon exhaust the hotel supply of the first grade. That this hotel should charge 3d per gallon less than hotels far less suitably situated for obtaining supplies is, I think, a reflection upon the proprietor's sense of fair trading.

The outbreak of war in August 1914 does not seem to have generated fears regarding the continuing supply of motor spirit. At the end of August, Shell announced that, in arrangement with the Society of Motor Manufacturers and Traders, no more than the following prices per gallon would be charged by their members to the public in England, Wales and Ireland: 'Shell' 1s 9d; 'Shell II' 1s 7d; and 'Crown' 1s 6d. Beyond Carlow, Mullingar and Arklow, the price was 1d more, and in the West 1¹/₂d more.

Shell products continued to be distributed by the British Petroleum Company Limited and although this arrangement apparently worked well, the outbreak of The Great War in August 1914 exposed the unlikely fact that the British Petroleum Company was German controlled. At first, when it seemed likely that the conflict would last no more than a few months, this was not a major problem and the status quo was maintained. However, as it became clear that no resolution to the conflict was likely in the short, or even the medium term, then this link became a major embarrassment to Shell. Indeed, Shell itself deemed it necessary to advertise widely that it had no German shareholders and that there was no German interest of any kind in the company and even to go as far as to offer a reward for information leading to the conviction of persons found libelling the Company! However, despite the outbreak of war, there was no legal way to end the British Petroleum Company contract which continued to have effect up until the end of 1916. As a result, plans were laid for a new company to take over the distribution of Shell products with effect from January 1st 1917 upon the expiry of the existing agreement with the British Petroleum Company.

With this in prospect, as early as January 1916, the Shell Marketing Company advertised for a manager to take charge of its Irish operations. The company also took a lease on spacious offices at No. 70 Grafton Street, Dublin, for use as its Irish headquarters.

Shell at the IAC Reliability Trial – 1913

The annual Reliability Trial of the Irish Automobile Club was the greatest test of motor cars in Ireland, comprising a series of reliability runs as well as hill-climbs throughout the country. It attracted enormous public interest and most of the top car manufacturers of the day entered teams. Those lucky enough to be successful widely advertised their achievements. Shell products were much in demand amongst the competitors and this solid-tyred truck with Shell product is shown supporting the 1913 event.

In due course, James Alexander Burns was appointed to look after the company's Irish interests. J A Burns was no stranger to the oil business, having represented the Homelight Oil Company in Ireland for a number of years. In February 1917, just after the new arrangement had come into effect, an article appeared in the Irish motoring magazine, the *Motor News*, recounting a visit to the company's Grafton Street premises and which provides us with a glimpse into its workings at that time.

> *Mr Burns gave us an insight into the wonderful organisation of the Shell Marketing Company. We have no hesitation in saying that we never came across any office in this country containing such up-to-date equipment. Mechanical calculation machines have been installed – machines to tot up long columns, to give you the square root of material, to tabulate, punch and check drivers' tickets. Perhaps the most interesting of these is the Elliot-Fisher typewriter for making out invoices and entering them in the ledger page at the same time. So far as our experience goes, this whole system is unique to the Irish motor trade. Notwithstanding the introduction of these up-to-date labour-saving devices, we found over forty clerks, male and female, employed at the Grafton Street offices. Mr Burns and his clever accountant, Mr A King, are to be heartily congratulated upon establishing such a splendid business organisation inside such a short period of time.*

The writer of this article also noted that *"already the company have fifteen travellers on the Irish ground, which fact can be taken as an index of very big business."* It also seems likely that most of the existing staff of the British Petroleum Company in Dublin simply moved over to the new Shell Marketing Company when it was established at the start of 1917. An interesting point made in the article was the company's intention, when the war was over, to make all their deliveries by lorry, and it was noted that they already *"have quite a large fleet, which will be augmented from time to time as*

James A Burns

Shell's first Irish Manager was James A Burns who took up his position on January 1st 1917. 'JA' Burns successfully steered the fledgling company through some of the most difficult years of its history during the War of Independence and the subsequent Civil War. He was succeeded by Captain Hugh St. G Harpur in 1930.

business grows." J A Burns was quoted as looking forward to the time when the horse will be *"relegated to the limbo of forgotten things."*

Clearly, from the foregoing, Shell was already a major force in the Irish market. And although there was a proliferation of small oil companies operating in the market, only one, the Anglo-American Oil Company Limited, which marketed petrol under the brand name 'Pratts', was of comparable size.

Shell's involvement in pioneering aviation came to the fore again in August 1919 when Captain John Alcock and Lieutenant Arthur Whitten Brown took off from Lester's Field near St. John's, Newfoundland, on the first non-stop flight by aeroplane across the Atlantic. They came to rest almost sixteen hours later in a *"soft Irish meadow"* near Clifden in Conne-mara. Their success was fêted world-wide and amongst many other honours, the modest duo were entertained by the Royal Irish Automobile Club at their Dawson Street premises – an event attended by Shell's senior Irish management.

On a more mundane level, one of the many issues facing the company at this time of great change was the return of 'Empties'. This had always been a problem but now, particularly because of wartime economies, it became vital to recover as many empty cans and steel barrels as possible from the trade. Widespread advertising campaigns were conducted to this end and

In a Soft, Irish Meadow …

Shell's involvement in pioneering aviation came to the fore in August 1919 when Captain John Alcock and Lieutenant Arthur Whitten Brown took off from Lester's Field near St. John's, Newfoundland, on the first non-stop flight by aeroplane across the Atlantic. They came to rest almost sixteen hours later in a "soft Irish meadow" which turned out to be a bog, near Clifden in Connemara. Their success was fêted world-wide and amongst many other honours, the modest duo were entertained by the Royal Irish Automobile Club at their Dawson Street, Dublin, premises – an event attended by Shell's senior Irish management.

31

credit was given on returned 'Empties' – a practice which was to continue for many years.

Soon, however, another altogether more serious issue was to arise.

It began in the middle of November 1919, when the Irish military authorities issued an Order prohibiting the having, keeping or using of a motor cycle or motorcar by civilians, without a naval, military or police permit. A similar order had already been in force for some time with regard to motor cycles and this was now cancelled, the new order covering both types of vehicle. Application for a permit in Dublin had to be made to the Metropolitan Police Superintendent of the Division in which the applicant resided while in other parts of Ireland the application was made to the District Inspector of the Royal Irish Constabulary. Fairly wide-ranging powers were given under the Order to any police constable who suspected it was being contravened and buildings could be entered and searched at any time of the day or night. A suspect vehicle could be seized and destroyed or disposed of by order of the Chief Officer of Police. In addition, infringements were punishable by a fine of £100 or six months imprisonment or both.

As so often seems to happen, officialdom got its wires crossed with regard to the introduction of the new Order, for although it came into effect on the 15th of November, the necessary permit application forms were unavailable until the end of that month. As a result, the Order was not enforced until the beginning of December.

In the meantime, the principal objections to the Order which had arisen from drivers were on the grounds that different (and harsher) legislation had been introduced for Ireland than for the rest of the United Kingdom and that some of the Irish Automobile Drivers and Mechanics' Union members, on political grounds, might be refused permits, and thus be prevented from following their trade. Deputation's to the Minister of Transport and the Lord Lieutenant of Ireland from many trade associations urged that the Order be modified before its introduction, but all appeals were ignored.

Within a week of the Order coming into force, a meeting was held of the Irish Automobile Drivers and Mechanics' Union at the Trades Hall in Capel Street, Dublin. The meeting decided that its members would not apply for the new Permit and support for this decision was received from the National Executive of the Irish Labour Party as well as the Trades Union Congress. The result of this decision to 'down tools' was quickly apparent as commercial vehicles disappeared off Irish streets and roads virtually overnight. Strangely, although the Order was the subject of extensive comment in the daily press,

Comment on the 'Permit' Strike

THE PETROL SHORTAGE
*Chauffeur: "Somebody has stolen the two-seater
while we've been away sir!"
Owner: "And the petrol?"
Chauffeur: "No, sir!"
Owner: "Thank God!"*

The Military Permit

No. 465   Not Transferable.

DEFENCE OF THE REALM REGULATIONS.

Age 21.

PERMIT for Driving **MOTOR CYCLE** or **MOTOR CAR** not the property of the
Holder of this Permit.

Height 5'8"

Mr. *Henry Ernest Bell* of *106 & 107 Mid. Abbey St.
Dublin*

Build *Medium.*

is hereby authorised to drive a Motor *Cars*
in respect of which a Permit is also held by Owner *Messrs Huet Bros,
106 & 107 Middle Abbey St., Dublin.*

Hair *Dark.*

Date *9th December 1919.*

Campbell Supt.

This Permit should be carried by the holder on Motor Cycle or Car, **together** with
Permit issued to Owner, and both Permits must be produced, on demand, to any Police
Constable.

If the holder of this Permit be a professional Motor Driver this Permit must only
be used when driving vehicles the property of his employer, as above, and must be sur-
rendered to the issuing Officer, in the event of any change of employer.

[OVER.

*The source of the widespread disturbance which came to be known as the 'Permit Strike' was the issue of permits by
the Military authorities prohibiting having, keeping or using of a motor cycle or motorcar by civilians, without a
naval, military or police permit. Many professional drivers believed that they would be prohibited from gaining
permits on political grounds, and thus would be prevented from following their trade.*

very few private motorists – who of course were similarly affected – added their voices to the howls of protest coming from other quarters.

A story was told in connection with the early days of the Permit Strike in the pages of the *Motor News* which says as much about the social mores of the time as it does about conditions which prevailed during the dispute:

Irish motorists are painfully aware that the Trades Union have put a ban on pleasure motoring, as a kind of sequel to the Permit Strike. Doctors and private owners generally are not interfered with, but the paid driver runs considerable risk if he takes out a car, as the roads around Dublin are pretty well picketed with strikers just at present. A friend of ours was anxious to take his chauffeur with him on a Christmas trip, but didn't fancy the risk involved in such an undertaking in these troublesome times. At length, a happy thought suggested itself to him. Why not dress him up as the owner of the car? The driver entered hugely into the joke, as he started off with fur coat, bowler hat at Beattie angle, collar, tie, and sporting pin. A fine shilling cigar completed the 'outfit', which we understand was most complete and successful in avoiding trouble. The camouflage was so perfect that two sets of pickets were passed without arousing the slightest suspicion...We are informed that there was no part of the joke the driver enjoyed better than the big 'Christmassy' cigar!

Whatever about such diversions, the Permit Strike soon reached serious proportions and before long spread as far as the handling and distribution of motor spirit. At the onset of the strike, the drivers of the motor vehicles used by the Anglo-American Oil Company and the Shell Marketing Company refused to take out their vehicles, but with the aid of horse-drawn transport, the two companies were able to maintain a level of supply close to their usual deliveries. But by the middle of January, the drivers of these vehicles as well as the workers in both company's filling departments had also joined the Strike. The inevitable consequence was that all deliveries of petrol ceased throughout Ireland. The strikers had initially given their own 'permits' to doctors so that they might continue their work, but this practice soon ceased. From around the country many unpleasant incidents were reported and the military authorities now intervened, taking control of the Alexandra Road storage depots of both Anglo-American and Shell as well as commandeering the motor lorries of both firms. A system was put in place whereby limited supplies of petrol were made available by the military authorities to persons *"having to discharge public or quasi-public duties."*

It soon became apparent that the authorities had no intention of

The First Annual Dinner Dance – 1920

The first Annual Dinner Dance of what was then the Irish Branch of the Shell Marketing Company, took place on Saturday, January 10th 1920, at a Dublin Hotel. Around 50 staff were in attendance and the central figure in the photograph is J A Burns, the Managing Director of Shell operations in Ireland. The event took place during the 'Permit' strike when the company was facing a significant crisis with regard to distribution of its products.

making any concession to the strikers and although the dispute dragged on for eleven weeks, it was doomed from the start to failure. Its collapse in the second week of February came about as a result of the intervention of Mr Harry Wayte of the well-known Dublin firm of A&B Taxies, which led to a statement by the Chief Commissioner of the Dublin Metropolitan Police clarifying the terms of the letter of application. This, in effect, relaxed several of the contentious conditions and allowed a number of weeks grace for drivers to complete the necessary paperwork to enable them to obtain their permit.

Thus, the drivers and filling staff of Shell returned to work and what was to prove to be the first of several 'military interventions' to ensure petrol supplies over the years came to an end.

While the crisis was at its height, on January 10th, Shell held its first annual dinner dance at a Dublin hotel attended by around fifty of the company's staff. Happily, the historic gathering was recorded by the camera, although the majority of faces look very serious, perhaps reflecting the uncertainties of the crisis facing the company.

Despite the restrictions placed on private and commercial motoring, the 1920 Royal Dublin Society Spring Show at the beginning of May was note-worthy for the large number of stands relating to transport and to the many possible uses of the internal combustion engine. Petrol or paraffin engines designed for practically every farm duty, from powering a small cream separator to heavy tractors of considerable power, were everywhere and as the market increased in its variety and scope, Shell was there too, displaying its range of fuels. Shortly after the company's successful participation at the RDS Show, the annual staff outing took place to Glendalough. The gathering consisted of the management and staff of the Grafton Street and North Wall offices together with the superintendents from the various districts through-out the country. Having travelled in two *char-a-bancs* hired especially for the occasion, the party lunched at the Royal Hotel, after which a sports programme consisting of racing, tug-o'-war and various novelty events took place on the open space in the vicinity of the Upper Lake. Mrs J A Burns, wife of the managing director, presented the prizes before the merry party returned via Roundwood and The Long Hill to Dublin.

Chapter 2

The 1920s:
Turbulent Times

SHELL joins the Irish Public in extending a cean rea rates to the gallant airmen who, in the face of appalling odds, accomplished the first East to West Atlantic Flight. Shell is proud of the part it played in the great adventure—proud that it was chosen when life and fame were at stake—proud that lubrication was perfectly satisfactory throughout the whole terrific test, and that the great engine of the Bremen was enabled to give of its best.

As with previous pioneering trans-Atlantic flights, Shell was involved with the flight of the Bremen in 1928.

1920-1929 Anglo-Irish Treaty signed – W T Cosgrave becomes first President of the Irish Free State – Irish Civil War – Discovery of Tutankhamun's tomb in Egypt – W B Yeats wins Nobel Prize for Literature – Shannon Scheme – 2RN, the predecessor of Radio Eireann, begins broadcasting – Economic slump – Mussolini and the Nazis emerge – Wall Street collapse

If the second decade of the century had been a turbulent one in which to do business in Ireland, then the advent of the new decade seemed only to promise more of the same. This turbulence intruded into the everyday social and business life of the community and R J Mecredy, Editor of the *Motor News*, recounted the following tale of a motoring trip with J A Burns during these times:

Motoring in Ireland is not altogether a bed of roses these days. We were out the other day with J A Burns, the Irish Manager of the Shell Marketing Company, on a short run in North County Dublin when we were stopped by two officers of the Royal Irish Constabulary who examined most carefully the driver's licence and the owner's permit.

In addition, our car was carefully searched for arms and ammunition, but the only 'arms' discovered took the form and shape of two hefty sets of golf clubs. Mr Burns produced a permit from General Boyd, Commanding officer for the district, enabling him to travel all over Ireland, remarking: "Did you ever see one of those before?" The officer examined it most critically, and in his best official manner said: "Now, tell me, for what reason did they give you that wide licence?" Herein we think he exceeded his duty somewhat. After all, it was none of his business as to why the permit was granted. Mr Burns courteously replied: "In order that the Irish motoring public might be kept well supplied with Shell motor spirit." We never like to criticise men who are doing a very unpleasant duty in a courteous way, but we do think that the seal and signature of the head of the military forces in Ireland ought to satisfy even the members of the R.I.C. without demanding the "why" and the "wherefore" as to the reason of any permit, however wide.

There was turbulence of a different kind when the price of petrol increased by an unprecedented 8d per gallon at the end of January 1920. Outraged motorists accused the petrol companies of making excessive profits and although Shell made a detailed and spirited defence explaining the reasons why it had been forced to make the increase, many motorists felt it was a case of, in the words of a catch-phrase then popular – *"Shell out again!"* No doubt, highly conscious of these feelings towards the petrol companies at this time, J A Burns was active on the committee (Irish Division – Southern) of the Motor Trade Association.

In July 1921, the company introduced a range of lubricants under the Shell brand onto the Irish market for the first time and these were extensively advertised alongside Shell Motor Spirit. Shell's business was growing steadily in Ireland. However, the establishment of the new Irish Free State in 1922 was a time of unprecedented uncertainty for all commercial enterprises, but most especially for businesses which were based abroad. Change and uncertainty went hand-in-hand and these proved difficult times for the company and its employees. Shell found its business in Ireland split by a border where none had existed before and some of the Dublin staff went north to assist in setting-up the Belfast office. The Civil War that followed the establishment of the Irish Free State affected the company's operations, sometimes in the most dramatic fashion, as during the burning of the Four Courts in Dublin, the incident that sparked off the Civil War, when a Shell Petrol lorry was commandeered from the Alexandra Road terminal at gun-point. In another incident, in which the ownership of the

Dangerous Times

A Shell lorry photographed in Rathdrum, County Wicklow, shortly before being commandeered at gun-point by 'Irregulars' during the Civil War in 1922.

Early Lorry Poster Advertising

A Shell Company lorry shod with solid tyres and with (from left) James Kelly (driver) with a Shell Mex dealer and his two children. The sides of these lorries had a panel which was used to paste up an advertising poster – in this case showing a pair of horses rearing with the message "A Perfect Power Pair, Shell Oil and Petrol." The photograph was taken around 1927.

vehicle concerned is not recorded, a tank wagon belonging to one of *"the leading distributing companies"* and containing a full load of motor spirit was stopped on a main road in County Kildare by a party of 'Irregulars' and the driver was forced at gun-point to drive to a quiet side-road. There the 'Irregulars' proceeded to use the contents of its tank to fill a full load of empty tins on a lorry already concealed there. Having completed their task, they saturated the tank wagon with a view to destroying it by fire. However, they overlooked the fact that in carrying the tins from the tank wagon to the lorry they had left a trail of spirit along the road. When a match was applied to the tank wagon, the flames at once extended to the lorry containing the newly-filled petrol tins, quickly reducing the wagon, the lorry and its contents to ashes.

However, despite these dangerous times, the company continued to grow and in 1922, a new company, Shell-Mex (Dublin) Limited, took over the interests of Shell and Eagle Oil in Southern Ireland, while the Irish BP Company Limited took over the interests of British Petroleum. (In December 1931, these two companies would be amalgamated as Shell and BP (Irish Free State) Limited, beginning an association which was to last until de-merger in 1976).

But even against this background of uncertainty, life went on for many much as it had always done. The early years of the new Irish Free State were hard times when a man or woman was glad to have work and a steady wage. A major feature of the company then was its still significant reliance on horse-drawn transport and one who remembered that difference was Paddy Finn who joined the company at the age of 16 in 1924 when he took over the Ballaghadreen Depot from his father, who was in ill health at the time. This early responsibility was made possible by the manager telling a white lie to Shell in London claiming he was 21! Paddy would help his father by looking after the horse, preparing his feed of bran mash with a pint of linseed oil every Saturday. The harness, too, demanded a lot of attention as it needed to be 'Brassoed' every two weeks. And when the majority of horses were finally phased out later in the 1920s, the trucks had to be washed every two weeks!

Another who had reason to remember the horse was Leo O'Carroll who joined Irish Shell in 1929. Leo recalled that one of his first jobs was to order the hay and nails for the horses and to check accounts for repairs to horses' harnesses. The significance of paraffin sales was also noted by Leo:

Paraffin was an extremely marketable commodity as people were coming from

A Roadside Site – 1920's

With the advent of Petrol pumps, then commonly known as petrol plants, the number of roadside filling stations throughout Ireland increased dramatically. These filling stations were, however, a long way removed from the model of what we are familiar with today, and tended to be either kerb-side sites or 'jack-of-all-trades' businesses where many items besides petrol were sold. This unidentified site was typical of many such sites.

the candle to the kerosene burner, with incandescent mantles and so on – the contrast being fantastic. Before that a draught could plunge a whole family into darkness so this was a great move forward.

Another who remembered those days was Jim Lynch who recalled joining Head Office in Dublin in the 1920s when his duties as a mailing clerk included collecting a can of milk in Duke Street for the afternoon tea. How things have changed!

By comparison with other employment available at the time, a job at Irish Shell was greatly prized and those fortunate enough to secure a position with the company counted themselves lucky in having a job they would stay loyal to for life. Conditions were, by comparison, very good and the company had clearly defined procedures for dealing with all eventualities. When a driver was operating a one man depot, separate instructions were issued on stocktaking, issue of receipts and transfer of moneys to Head Office by way of postal order. As a driver salesman, he was frequently reminded of his responsibilities to increase sales all year round. Comparative figures on record show that company drivers earned between 25% and 30% more than the average for lorry drivers at the time. Pump fitters were extremely well paid in the 1920s and the records show a weekly wage of £4 15s 0d (£4.75) to a new recruit in 1926. Shopkeepers and clerical staff were on much lower rates earning as little as 25s (£1.25) per week in the 1930s.

In 1926, the foundations of what was to be a long-lasting and successful relationship were established. James Gowan McMullan and William McMullan, together with their associate W W Kennedy, had first established their oil business in 1917. Initially, they purchased their petroleum requirements from the Anglo-Mexican Oil Company, and when this company was taken over by Shell in 1926, they began to draw their supplies from Irish Shell. Today, McMullan's have an extensive network of company-owned stations and dealers throughout the 32 counties of Ireland and continues to draw supplies from Irish Shell.

From its very first advertisement in Ireland in 1906, Shell had successfully sold the brand 'Shell' and created a distinctive style which over the next two decades became instantly recognisable and which contrasted greatly with the advertising of its principal competitors. As the mid-point of the 1920s approached, this 'Shell' advertising style became even more distinctive and assured. Although the golden age of Shell advertising was still some years in the future, many memorable campaigns were developed in the 1920s, particularly notable being those incorporating the drawings of

McMullan's and Shell – A long Association

James Gowan McMullan

The business of McMullan Brothers was first established in 1917 by James Gowan McMullan and William McMullan together with their associate W W Kennedy. They initially purchased their petroleum requirements from the Anglo-Mexican Oil Company, and when this company was taken over by Shell in 1926, they began what has been a long association with Irish Shell, from whom they continued to draw supplies. Today, trading under the Maxol brand, McMullan's have an extensive network of company owned stations and dealers throughout the 32 counties of Ireland.

William McMullan

43

H E Bateman and also a series of testimonial advertisements by prominent motoring journalists of the time. The 'Bateman' campaign is sheer magic. Assured, memorable and simple in execution it gave to Shell a brand-leader stance it was never to lose in the Irish market. The series of testimonial advertisements – a format to which we have grown accustomed today – was prepared at a time when the motoring public was strongly influenced by first-hand recommendation and when the imprimatur of these prominent motoring journalists was highly persuasive – in a much less cynical age – in building allegiance to the Shell brand. And although the bulk of Shell advertising at this time originated in London, more and more local variations of their central themes began to be produced by the company's new Irish Advertising Agency, McConnells, with whom Shell was to have a long and fruitful relationship. (These themes are explored in more detail in Appendix 1 – The Golden Age of Shell Advertising).

One aspect of the company's advertising didn't, however, receive the widespread approval of the Irish public. Particularly in the years following the end of the War, petrol advertising signs had begun to appear all over the Irish countryside as motorised travel became more common. Completely unregulated, these signs were at first a novelty but quickly became an eyesore in a landscape previously almost unsullied by intrusive advertising signs. In response to a growing public outcry, the petroleum companies undertook to remove these signs in 1924, an event Shell turned to its advantage in the following advertisement:

Shell in the North West

Irish Shell driver Bill Scally photographed with his Lorry
at Eyrecourt, County Galway.

The first delivery of petrol to Paddy Bonner's Filling Station at Gweedore, County Donegal, c. 1929. The driver on the right is Charlie Moore from Letterkenny and his helper is Charlie Sweeney from Crolly.

Around this time, the editor of the *Motor News* reported that J A Burns, Shell-Mex Managing Director in Ireland, while motor boating in Dublin Bay, had slipped on deck and fractured an ankle. *"It is rather hard luck on such an active man to have to resort to crutches, the slowest form of locomotion, on the eve of his holidays. With his usual good spirits, 'J.A.' hopes to carry on. Meanwhile, for a month at least, it is a case of good-bye to golf and fishing, his two favourite hobbies".* 'J.A.' was indeed a keen sportsman, and his love of golf was reflected when in 1926 he presented a silver trophy to the company to be competed for in an annual golf competition. Happily, today, the 'J. A. Burns Cup' is still competed for annually and is a most prized award.

The first kerb-side petrol pump in Ireland was introduced at 25 Nassau Street, Dublin, in 1923, and these had rapidly multiplied so that, by 1928, the installation of petrol pumps was widespread throughout the country. Prior to this the vast bulk of petrol sales had been from general stores who sold petrol in two gallon cans. This 'Can Trade' was to remain an important element of Shell's business in Ireland up until the mid-1930s. Now, however, with the growth of petrol pump numbers, Shell found it necessary to take action against a practice which had become commonplace, when it successfully prosecuted a local garage proprietor at Swinford Court for selling motor spirit to which the trade-mark Shell-Mex was falsely applied. A Shell representative stopped his car at the defendant's pump, asked for four gallons of 'Shell', got fuel from the 'Shell' pump and received a receipt on which the word 'Shell' was written. On analysis, the petrol turned out to be an inferior grade to any Shell product on sale in the country. During the case, which received widespread coverage, it became apparent that the practice was commonplace. The Justice found for Shell and the defendant was fined £3 with £7 costs. The case kept the letter-writers to the papers busy for many weeks and Shell-Mex was widely congratulated for taking a stand on the issue, which it was felt had brought discredit and suspicion to the Irish Motor trade.

Coincidentally, shortly after this case, the Minister for Industry and Commerce, Mr P McGilligan, introduced a Weights and Measures Bill to the Dáil which for the first time made provision for the inspection and testing of petrol pumps at garages. As many of the existing pumps didn't meet the standards laid down in the Bill, an exemption allowed the older pumps to continue for a specified period. During the course of the passage of the Bill through the Dáil, it was stated that of the eighty million gallons of petrol sold in the Irish Free State during 1927, seventy per cent had been dispensed through pumps.

Staff at Sligo Depot – 1927

*Staff at the Shell depot in Sligo photographed in 1927 included
(from left) T Rooney, T Rooney, J Callaghan, P Doherty (storekeeper),
J Jenkins and M Rooney (driver).*

In April 1928, Shell became a part of the first East to West non-stop flight across the Atlantic when it supplied lubricants to the *Bremen*. This German monoplane was crewed by Captain Hermann Koehl, Baron von Huenefeld and an officer of the Irish Army Air Corps, Commandant James Fitzmaurice. The trio took off from Baldonnel aerodrome on April 28th and after an epic flight lasting some thirty-six and a half hours landed on Greenly Island, on the coast of Labrador. The wave of enthusiasm which followed their return to Dublin where they were enthusiastically fêted led to the establishment of a new Irish Aero Club which helped to train a number of amateur pilots during the succeeding years.

The following month, Shell-Mex (Ireland) continued its long established support of the Royal Dublin Society's annual Spring Show. Its 1928 stand in the capable hands of J A Burns and Captain Harpur seems to have been a particularly special effort and gained much favourable comment from the Press.

With the ending of the Civil War in 1923, and the establishment of the Cumann na nGaedheal political party by W T Cosgrave who had supported the Anglo-Irish Treaty of 1921, the new State set out, somewhat shakily it must be said, on the democratic road. Cosgrave led his party into government and was to remain in power until 1932. Beset by a myriad of difficulties, there was little good news emanating from the new State. Prior to the War, Ireland had, largely through the writings of R J Mecredy, been slowly developing as a tourist destination. The conflicts of the intervening years had all but destroyed this prospect, and so it was with some enthusiasm that the Cosgrave Government welcomed the proposal of the Royal Irish Automobile Club to stage an international motor race in Dublin's Phoenix Park during 1929. Conscious of the highly successful Tourist Trophy races first organised by the Ulster Automobile Club at the Ards circuit in 1928, Cosgrave and his government welcomed the opportunity to bring large numbers of visitors as well as the World's Press to Dublin for the race. Titled the Irish International Grand Prix, the event was to be a two-day event, with the Saorstat Cup race for sports cars under 1500cc on the Friday and the Eireann Cup race for sports cars over 1500cc on the Saturday. The winner of the Irish International Grand Prix Trophy would be the driver who completed either race at the fastest speed. Thus, in line with Shell's international commitment to motor sport, Shell-Mex (Ireland) found itself involved in servicing the fuel and lubricant needs of several of the leading teams participating in the event. The Irish International Grand Prix turned out to be a resounding success and was won by the White Russian *émigré*,

The Flight of the *Bremen*

In April 1928, the Atlantic was crossed successfully for the first time in an East/West direction by a heavier-than-air aircraft. The crew (from left) consisted of Captain Herman Koehl, Colonel James C Fitzmaurice and Baron Von Huenefeld. The trio became international heroes following the success of their endeavour – one of the greatest of pioneering flights in Aviation's rich history. Fuel for the flight was supplied by BP Ireland and lubricants by Irish Shell.

49

Boris Ivanowski driving an Alfa Romeo. For Shell, the result was a great success with the first six fastest cars all using Shell Oil and Petrol – a fact which the company widely advertised.

The race and its organisation by the Royal Irish Automobile Club with the backing of the Free State Government was internationally acclaimed and the meeting was held again in 1930 and 1931 before a change of government and consequent loss of support for the Club's efforts led to its abandonment in 1932. The 1930 race proved to be the highlight of the series and was contested by most of the great drivers of the day. Fittingly, it was the young German sensation, Rudolph Caracciola, who triumphed in a sensational race, driving a Mercedes SSK. Once again, Shell products were used by the winning team – as indeed, they were also in 1931 when Norman Black triumphed driving the Earl of March's MG Midget, although there was some bad feeling when a rival company also claimed to have supplied fuel to the winning team. This was subsequently firmly dismissed in follow-up Shell advertising.

As a footnote to the victory in 1930, a young teenage boy present at the race and one of those who fêted the winning driver was later to achieve his ambition of working for Shell-Mex. Incredibly, some sixty years later, Arthur Henderson was to see for the first time a photograph of himself with the victorious Caracciola in the Irish Shell retail magazine *Shell People*, recalling an unforgettable day from his teenage years.

Shell's involvement with the Irish International Grand Prix was to herald the beginning of a long tradition of involvement with all aspects of Irish motorsport, but particularly with motor racing in the Phoenix Park, which continued for many years afterwards.

The end of the decade saw a number of significant changes as the company moved from its Head Office at Grafton Street to new accommodation at No. 21 Dame Street, over Burton's, the well-known tailors, a modern office building with greatly increased accommodation for the rapidly growing numbers of staff. At the same time, J A Burns, who had been with the company since 1917, retired and was replaced by Captain Hugh St. G Harpur, who had joined the company in 1922 following service in the British Army and a period with Harry Ferguson's Dublin garage at Baggot Street.

Captain Hugh St. G. Harpur

Captain Harpur succeeded James Burns as Managing Director in 1930 and remained in the position until 1948 – a longer period than any other managing director of the company before or since. An ex-army officer, he joined Shell-Mex (Dublin) Limited, as it was titled then, in 1922.

Shell Voices

Life as a Junior Clerk

I joined the British Petroleum Company in April 1919 as a junior clerk. My salary was 12 shillings (60p) a week. The office was situated on East Wall Road in Dublin. Most of the workers had to walk to work. The nearest tram passed by Annesley Bridge in Fairview. The staff brought in lunch, made tea and had a snack for their mid-day meal. I lived in Henry Street at the time, and had to walk each way four times a day. Also being office junior, I had to do various messages.

Albert Fitzell, who joined British Petroleum in 1919 and later worked for Irish Shell and BP.

Early Managers at Foynes

Our first Installation Manager
His name was John McVeigh,
He ruled and trained all the staff
In the methods of the day.
From Nineteen-o-four to nineteen twelve
Trade developed fast
Then one day he was called away
To charge up in Belfast

Number two was a cooperage foreman
John O'Connell was his name.
From nineteen twelve to twenty-four
He held the guiding rein.
Those were the days of the wood-barrelled oil trade,
And rail tank cars as well
Those were BP days for all railways
So old times tell.

Number three was N E O'Story
For a time he was Resident Engineer
Supervising erection of tanks
C.D.E.F. and laying pipelines to the pier.
Installation Manager he then became
In nineteen twenty-four.
In nineteen twenty-six he went to Trieste
We saw him never more.
Number four was G Fitzmahoney
His term was short indeed
In nineteen twenty-seven
He was called to Heaven,
May he rest in peace.

The Irish International Grand Prix

Reproduced by kind permission of An Post ©

The three Irish International Grand Prix held in Dublin's Phoenix Park between 1929 and 1931 were a huge success for the young Irish Free State and were internationally acclaimed for the organisation of the Royal Irish Automobile Club and for the superb racing they produced. The highlight was the 1930 race, won by the young German star, Rudolph Caracciola. His win, driving a Mercedes SSK in wet conditions was recalled in Vincent Killowry's fine painting which was the subject of an An Post stamp issue in 2001. In the photograph, Caracciola is fêted after his famous win. Incidentally, the young lad just to the left of Caracciola is a teenage Arthur Henderson, who almost a decade later, went to work for Irish Shell.

Number five was a County Cork man
Dick Walsh was his name
For eighteen years to forty-six,
A record service of fame.
He saw the first of the flying boats
Arranged for re-fuelling same
She was owned by Imperial Airways
Cambria was her name.

Number six was Frank Smith
He replaced Dick Walsh
Number seven was Leo O'Carroll
The last of the Managers here.

Patrick P O'Connell, who served with Shell and British Petroleum between 1915 and 1929 and also between 1944 and 1958

Oil Deliveries

The oil was delivered from bulk tank wagons which carried 500 gallons and were drawn by two horses. There were two five-gallon cans hanging on two taps at the back of the large tank. It was from these that the drivers made the deliveries of paraffin oil to small shops, who sold it in small quantities to customers who used it in oil lamps, which most people had for lighting their houses. The other mode of fuel was gas, which was supplied by the Dublin Gas Company. There was no electricity in those days. This didn't come for many years after. BP had about fifty depots all over the country. These were usually situated at the railway stations in large towns. The oil was stored in large tanks which were fed from rail cars sent from Dublin installation at Alexandra Road.

Albert Fitzell, who joined British Petroleum in 1919 and later worked for Irish Shell and BP.

The Road Tank Wagon and its Driver

The road tank wagon we used to see
In the good old bygone days
It was painted green and in gold
Was letters 'Royal Standard and White May'.
In fancy now I see it go
Drawn by a chestnut pair
With shining harness and tingling bells
Out on the sales each day.
A load four hundred gallons of oil
The price was not considered dear
Would be sold in Askeaton, Newcastle, Rathkeale,
By O'Sullivan from Ardineer.

From the Past ...

Retired Irish Shell driver, Jackie McGettigan, is pictured with the late Jim Kennedy of the Donegal Oil Company, at the opening of the new Shell Ramelton Service Station in 1995. The occasion was also the first appearance of Jackie's newly restored Shell delivery truck. Dating from 1929, the truck is the result of a huge amount of careful and painstaking restoration work carried out by Jackie over many years.

He was driver and salesman all on his own,
The first for the old BP.
Westward he went to Ballyhahill and Glin,
Tarbert and Turraree.
And East to Shanagolden, Newcastle,
Rathkeale, Askeaton and Ballysteen.

Tho' his area small and his speed was slow,
Compared with the present way
Those steeds jogged on, the old wagon rolled along
Out on the sales each day
And always sold a wagon load
Of 'Royal Standard' and 'White May'.
For many years he drove those steeds
Groomed and fed them well
Stabled at night and bedded
'Twas he could do it so well.
But came a day when those two chestnut bays
And the old tank wagon too
Were taken away for good and aye
And replaced by the motor new.

Patrick P O'Connell, who served with Shell and British Petroleum between 1915 and 1929 and also between 1944 and 1958

Why the Kero storage was always short!
I recall twenty-five years happy service at Dublin installation before going to Head Office for another twenty years. During my time at Dublin Depot, we had one horse drawn cart holding a 200 gallon tank (kerosene). The driver was an expert in backing that cart under the small kerosene filling arm. In examining the concrete under the filling arm, I found a small dent or groove where the driver went to great pains in having the rear wheel of his van, thus giving him an extra few gallons of kero to sell in the shops round Sheriff Street. He was most annoyed when this was rectified (the kero storage was always short). We only had one bulk lorry (an Albion) with solid rubber front wheels. The two Leyland lorries kept a carpenter more or less full-time boring holes in the floor boards to suit the different 2000 and 3000 gallon tanks. Yet with such a makeshift fleet, we did most of the trade in Dublin and its suburbs. The 'Depot' consisted of a corrugated hut about 10' x 6' which held four staff and we had to pack paper in the cracks to keep out the elements. Head Office was over the Singer Sewing Machine shop in Grafton Street (long since gone). When I see the new Dublin installation and Head Office at Beech Hill, I'm afraid I was born too soon.

Sam Pullen – Head Office Administration

A familiar Sight

Through the 1920s and into the 1930s the horse-drawn Shell and BP Delivery Wagons, a familiar sight throughout the length and breath of Ireland, gradually gave way to motorised Delivery lorries. This BP example was photographed in Upper Main Street, Letterkenny around 1936.

Branding the Horses

I remember some of the drivers delivering oil to the fishing boats at Howth, often got a present of fish from the fishermen, which they brought home and distributed amongst the staff at no cost. Horses were numbered with branding irons which were sent out to the depots by post whenever there was a change of animal. This would occur when an animal had fallen and broken a leg and had to be destroyed.

Albert Fitzell, who joined British Petroleum in 1919 and later worked for Irish Shell and BP.

Tea vouchers and House loans

When I joined the company in 1928, there was no overtime and anyone who had to work late was given a tea voucher for 1s 9d. At that time the company made house loans to staff at 1¹/₂% interest.

Frank Flood (In a recollection recorded in 1983) – Head Office Administration

Life as the 'Dogs-body'

Ernie and Joe Doyle were employed as first and second boys, and as I came in last, I was the junior and 'dogs-body'. Ernie and Joe were eventually promoted and new boys brought in. We had to take it in turns to post all the mail at O'Connell Street by 6 o'clock sharp. The mail was carried in a large leather bag, which was about three foot square. I had to work six days a week and also attend Maguire's Civil Service College in O'Connell Street five nights a week from 7 o'clock to 9 o'clock to finish my education. We left school in those days around 14 years of age. As I lived at 56 Henry Street (which is now Roche's Stores), I can tell you that I was very tired when the day was finished.

Albert Fitzell, who joined British Petroleum in 1919 and later worked for Irish Shell and BP.

Disappearing Labels!

At around the start of the Northern Ireland troubles , BP bought over Rathborne's Candle factory and wanted to send a couple of hundred cases to Belfast. They didn't want to send them with Southern labels, so it was decided to have new labels printed suitable for the North of Ireland. Joe Doyle and myself were told to go down to the East Wall Road stable yard and re-label all the cases. We cycled down and pasted the new labels on the cases which were stacked along the yard four high, and went back to the office and reported that the job was completed. The following morning, Joe and I were called in by the accountant and asked why we didn't label all the cases. While we were there, the phone rang. It was the storeman to say that one of the drivers told him that he had seen the stableman's goat eating the labels off the cases. It appears that goats will eat practically anything, and when he got the taste of the labels, which were pasted on with flour paste, he just kept going! Needless to say, this caused much amusement among the staff in the office.

Albert Fitzell, who joined British Petroleum in 1919 and later worked for Irish Shell and BP.

Moloney's of Abbeyfeale

Typical of filling sites in provincial Ireland in the 1920s and '30s was J F Moloney's at Abbeyfeale in County Limerick. The size of these early petrol pumps is startling when compared to today's equivalent as is their positioning on the kerb-side – a practice once commonplace but which has almost disappeared today.

Chapter 3

The 1930s:
Putting Down Roots

SHELL & "BP" (I.F.S.)LTD

The short-lived logo of Shell & BP (Irish Free State) Limited. The company came into being in 1931 and changed its name to Irish Shell Limited in 1933.

1930-1939 Eamon de Valera becomes Taoiseach – Eucharistic Congress – Economic War – Car assembly begins in Irish Free State – Inaugural Aer Lingus flight – First traffic lights in Dublin – Anglo-Irish Agreement – 'Irish Free State' becomes 'Eire' – New constitution introduced – The Emergency begins

Following the move of the company's headquarters in 1930, at the end of the following year, Shell-Mex (Dublin) Limited and Irish B.P. Limited merged to become Shell and BP (Irish Free State) Limited.

Upon this merger, the new company rationalised its depot system and concentrated on three water-fed bulk plants at Dublin, Cork and Foynes. Captain Hugh St. G Harpur came to be Managing Director of Shell-Mex (Ireland) at a time of great change. The new state had overcome many of its early difficulties and a new confidence and self-belief was abroad in the country. This was reflected in 1932 when Harpur employed a plane to undertake a tour of inspection of the company's depots and installations. A contemporary publication reported:

That ever-progressive concern, Messrs. Shell and BP (I.F.S.) Limited can always be relied upon to keep well abreast of the times. During the past week they have been using a Puss Moth aeroplane for the purpose of enabling the

61

managing director, Captain Hugh Harpur, to make a tour of inspection of the company's depots in the Free State. The 'plane was to have been flown over from England in time for the Athy air pageant last Sunday week but was held up by bad weather at the week-end. Captain Harpur's pilot was Captain Taylor, and Colonel C F Russell accompanied him. The tour lasted four days, during which fifteen landings were made. As a result of the tour much useful information in regard to landing grounds throughout the country was made available. This is stated to be the first example of the use of an aeroplane in this country for an ordinary business object. It resulted in a great saving of time.

The Shell Company has always taken a great interest in the development of aviation in Ireland, and some years ago materially assisted the first air mail flight between England and Ireland.

It would appear that Captain Harpur developed an interest in aviation and he was to be found associated with various significant aviation developments in Ireland over the succeeding years. Colonel Charles F Russell, who accompanied Captain Harpur on the tour of inspection, had earlier been the pilot of the first mail plane to fly from Galway to London (via Dublin) to demonstrate the value of linking by air a trans-Atlantic liner calling at Galway with London. Shortly afterwards Russell joined McConnell's Advertising Service, and on October 22nd 1932, Russell also organised the second stage of this demonstration which was to pick up mail from Galway, fly it to Dublin and then on by a larger aircraft to Berlin. The aircraft used was a three-engined Fokker monoplane of Royal Dutch Airlines (KLM) carrying sixteen passengers. This flight attracted enormous publicity – even more than many of the trans-Atlantic flights – and Captain Harpur and Shell were once again involved.

Colonel Russell was a most interesting character and had been a wartime fighter pilot with the Royal Flying Corps. It was he who organised the purchase of an aeroplane to use in case a speedy getaway was required by Michael Collins and three others from the Treaty negotiations in London, and in due course he became the second-in-command of the newly formed Free State Air Force. Later in the 1930s, he would also become a director of Irish Shell Limited.

Russell's demonstration flight focused attention on the West coast of Ireland as a site for an airport and several surveys were carried out including one by Sir Alan Cobham, who was later to have two more links with Ireland and Shell – as the head of the first 'Air Circus' to visit this country, and

Pioneering Irish Aviation

Captain Hugh St G Harpur maintained Irish Shell's position as a supporter of many of the great aviation pioneering flights. In the top photograph, Captain Harpur is pictured in the door of the first Galway to Berlin Flight in 1932 upon arrival at Croydon en-route. The others pictured are (from left) S Dunkley, J Dulanty, High-Commissioner Irish Free State, Colonel C F Russell who later became a director of Irish Shell and Charles E McConnell, Managing Director of McConnell's Advertising Service.

Also in 1932, Capt. Harpur became the first to use an aeroplane for ordinary business purposes in Ireland when he used a DH Puss Moth to undertake a tour of inspection of the company's sites throughout the country. The pilot was Captain Taylor and they were accompanied by Colonel C F Russell.

subsequently (after the introduction of regular trans-Atlantic services by flying-boat) as the managing director of Flight Refuelling, the organisation which pioneered the satisfactory refuelling of aircraft in flight.

This was a period of steady expansion for the company and recruitment for driving staff, particularly in country areas, depended greatly on references from business people or previous employers who were customers of the company. Wages in the early 1930s ranged from £2 5s 0d (£2.25) to £3 5s. 0d (£3.25), often depending on the weight of the truck, e.g. a 1¹/₂ ton Ford to a 2¹/₂ ton Dennis. Wage increases required a formal recommendation from the Branch and Divisional Sales Managers. One unfortunate driver who hadn't found favour with his superiors was granted an increase of 2/6 (12.5p) per week after three years service and a further 5/- (25p) for improved performance – but only after a further four years – his wage amounting to £3 7s 6d (£3.37) in 1935.

Many jobs were done 'by the book' and it is interesting to read the written instructions issued to all the company's drivers in 1930. These included the following edicts:

Tyres: Where inflated tyres are fitted to a vehicle these should be checked each morning for correct pressure, stone cuts and small flints which may become embedded in the tyre.

Clutch: At least ³/₄" free travel is required for the effective operation of the clutch. If your inspection reveals a lesser amount you must not take the vehicle on the road but must notify Head Office by the quickest means available to you.

Battery: You should check the level in the cells each week and fill as necessary with distilled water. If you cannot purchase distilled water locally, then carry out the following procedure. Place an earthenware vessel in the open to collect rainwater (never off the roofs of buildings). Wash two glass corked bottles and when sufficient water has been collected pour it into the bottles and thus maintain a suitable supply of water for use in batteries.

A separate leaflet is enclosed describing in detail the manner in which you must wash the vehicle at least once a week.

By 1935 the company's name had changed once again. This time the company became simply Irish Shell Limited, dropping the reference to B.P. from its title. A note accompanying the release of the company's 1935

Flying the Mails and Cobham's Air Circus

Irish Shell played an important role in most of the pioneering flights originating in Ireland between the wars. The top photograph shows the Fokker Monoplane being refuelled during its flight to demonstrate a link between Galway and Berlin, via Dublin where the photograph was taken. The plane carried mail and 16 passengers including the Irish Shell Managing Director, Captain Harpur.

Air 'Circuses' helped to generate public enthusiasm for aviation in the 1930s by visiting provincial districts. Here, (on right) Geoffrey Tyson's Avro Cadet is refuelled at a temporary airfield during its Irish tour in 1933. The final photograph shows an Airspeed Ferry used to give 'joy-rides' by Sir Alan Cobham's Circus in 1933.

Report included some interesting statistics. It claimed that Irish Shell was the largest distributive organisation of any kind in the Free State. It had 3 ocean installations, 28 main depots and 38 sub-depots, a fleet of 73 rail cars and 209 road vehicles. A sum of over £12,000 was paid in road taxation annually while railway freight cost the company over £64,000 per annum. A similar note to the 1936 Report further illuminates the company's importance within the Free State economy. To the above was added the information that a sum of £107,000 was paid out in wages. More than half the share capital of £220,000 was held by Irish nationals and the directorate and management was entirely controlled by Irishmen.

In addition to these directly calculable figures could be added the employment brought about by the production of Irishell Benzole mixture. For this interesting experiment, ultimately a failure, the Benzole content was produced at the plant of the Dublin Gas Company and blended with petrol at the Irish Shell works at North Wall, Dublin.

During this period, Irish Shell came under the control of George Wilson, who was very much the crown-prince-in-waiting to Shell-Mex BP's (SMBP) first chief, F L Halford. Together with aviation, in which he had also no interest, Halford handed over complete responsibility for Ireland to Wilson, leaving him entirely to his own devices in these matters.

Writing in the excellent 'SMBP History' published by the 44 Club in 1999, John Higdon tells the following story:

Ireland fascinated Wilson as it had many of the qualities of life that he enjoyed. There was of course the fishing and he was also an artist manqué and much appreciated the bohemian way of life. He himself told the story that, on his first visit to Dublin, the assorted turf bank operators and race horse owners who made up the sales force were summoned to meet the big white chief from England. The General Manager, Hugh St. G Harpur, sat at a table with two assistants and a bottle of John Powers from which he took an invigorating swig to start proceedings. He introduced Wilson who would now give them a message from on high. After a sentence or two his flow was interrupted by a hoarse voice "Oh, 'tis cock he is talking". A reproving voice "Tim, Tim, you must not say cock to Mr Wilson". Unrepentant voice "But it is cock that he is talking". The awkward situation was saved by the doors of the hall being flung open and a functionary called "Bhoys, they are open". The multitude with one accord wheeled round and left the hall. George Wilson was left to savour his Irish baptism while Hugh St. G Harpur reached out for another John Powers.

Irishell – An Interesting Experiment

In 1935 the company launched 'Irishell' – a blend of Benzole supplied by the Alliance and Dublin Consumers Gas Company (who erected a new plant for its blending) and petrol from Irish Shell. The new product was given the unlikely name of 'Irishell' – pronounced 'Iri-shell' – and launched amid a fanfare of advertising, two of the press advertisements being shown above. However, it failed to find acceptance from the Irish motoring public and quietly faded away after a couple of years.

One suspects that this is a story that grew somewhat in the course of repeated re-telling.

In 1936 the legislation which, in part, at least, was the fruit of the early experimental Atlantic flights was passed by the Oireachtas as the Air Navigation and Transport Act. International agreements regarding the operation of the North Atlantic Air Service followed and work began on the construction of the international airport at Rineanna. The task was huge and involved the draining of 760 acres of land and the construction of the first concrete runways which would take some six years to complete.

In the meantime, only flying-boats had the range and safety margins for trans-Atlantic crossings, and it was decided that the survey flights by both American and British companies should be undertaken by this type of aircraft. Foynes, located on the south bank of the Shannon, was chosen as the Irish base for these operations. Like the site chosen for the new airport, Rineanna, it had a remarkably good record of being free from poor weather. In addition it had an already existing good quay and Shell had a substantial oil installation already sited there. It was just 25 miles from Limerick. Radio facilities for communications and direction-finding were established in the neighbourhood and temporary control offices were established in the rooms above the bar in the Monteagle Arms Hotel. A refuelling barge for flying-boats had to be designed and Tom Crawford Young and Mick Finnucane – the harbour pilot at Foynes – after weighing up the options, purchased a converted ship's lifeboat in Waterford and had it taken to Arklow where the work was carried out in John Tyrrell's shipyard.

A Shell publication *Flights of Memory* produced in 1956, described the activity thus:

Many strangers visited Foynes, and people who had never heard of this quiet little Limerick village began to read its name in their morning newspapers...much romantic nonsense was written, but the basic project – in the Summer of 1937 – was a trail-blazing flight which represented the first step taken on this side of the Atlantic by a commercial company (at that time Imperial Airways) for the establishment of a regular air service between the Old World and the New.

It was not a romantic adventure, as the early trans-Atlantic flights had been: it was the culmination of several years intensive work by aviation experts on both sides of the Atlantic, and the scheme was divided into three stages.

The first was the survey and experimental flights – planned by Imperial

Golf Outing – 1935

The 1935 Irish Shell Golf Outing took place at Woodbrook, County Dublin on June 27th. The main award, the Burns Cup was won by (top photo, left) J Doherty. Also in the photograph is Captain Harpur, Managing Director and Senator T V Honan, winner of the captain's prize.
In the lower photograph are pictured some of the staff of Irish Shell who attended the outing at Woodbrook.

Airways and Pan-American Airways: second, the operation of a mail service; and third, the passenger services which operate regularly at the present time.

The *Caledonia*, one of 28 Empire-type flying-boats owned by Imperial Airways, was scheduled with its sister-plane, the *Cambria*, for the survey flights, additional fuel tanks having been installed in both aircraft and all passenger accommodation removed. Piloted by Captain Arthur S Wilcockson, *Caledonia* made a successful flight from Foynes to Port Botwood, then on to Montreal and New York. In the reverse direction the Sikorsky *Clipper III*, piloted by Captain Harold Gray, arrived successfully at Foynes and then flew on to Southampton.

As was recorded in *Flights of Memory*:

The headlines grew smaller – trans-ocean survey flights became a routine matter, of concern in this country apparently only to the personnel at Foynes...That, in itself, was an achievement: it took Atlantic flying out of the romantic stage, it is now an everyday business.

Two years later – on the eve of World War II – regular scheduled trans-Atlantic services were formally started from Foynes on August 6th 1939 when the flying-boat *Caribou* piloted by Irishman, Captain J C Kelly-Rogers, departed for Boucherville. The first American commercial flight took place a month later. Over the next few years, Foynes, and Shell, would play a pivotal role in the development of trans-Atlantic passenger travel.

Several other experimental flights involving Shell facilities at Foynes also took place during this period. The most intriguing of these was the Composite plane – the mail-carrying seaplane *Mercury* which was carried to operating height on the back of the flying-boat *Maia*. Perhaps of more significance were the experiments carried out when a tanker-plane took off from the partially completed Rineanna and flew over the Shannon where it refuelled a flying-boat in mid-air enabling it to make its journey across the Atlantic carrying a greater payload.

However, gathering storm clouds on the European horizon were to change the nature of the operation at Foynes, although the flying-boats were to continue to use its facilities for a further number of years. The outbreak of War in Europe was followed by Ireland's declaration of neutrality and the period which came to be known as 'The Emergency'. Once again, conflict had overtaken the development of Shell's business in Ireland and would have a profound effect on the events of the next decade.

Flying-Boats at Foynes

The Imperial Airways Shorts S.23 Flying-Boat Caribou, *in the course of being refuelled by one of the Shell boats at Foynes just prior to the Second World War. The boats were SHELLEIRE (1,200 gallons capacity) and SHELLAVIA (1,000 gallons capacity). The fuel was stored at the Foynes installation which in turn was supplied by coastal tankers from the UK. Fuel was delivered by motor tanker from the Foynes installation to the two boats at Foynes pier. Painting by Vincent Killowry.*

Shell Voices

Lorry Boy

In December 1934, as a schoolboy aged 15 years, I recall the Shell Driver, Paddy Madden, making one of his periodic deliveries of Kerosene to my Aunt's shop to refill her 10 gallon drum. On that particular occasion, he asked her if she could spare me for the Christmas holidays. "You may take him away", *she replied. From these simple origins, there began a career for me which spanned 35 years with Irish Shell.*

I was initially employed as a Lorry Boy and was informed that this employment would cease at age 18. However, on reaching this cut-off point, it so happened that the depot clerk in Limerick was transferred to Galway on promotion, which created a vacancy in Limerick depot. I was well enough regarded by then to be called into the office and given a test and interview for the position. Having succeeded in this I was duly appointed.

John 'Sean' McMahon, Lorry Boy and Driver.

Through no fault of your own ...

I was one of three lads in the Mailing Department under the control of a member of the 'Corps of Commissionaires' called Mr Wilding, a formidable ex-British army man with only one arm which whacked around our ears on occasions. We handled all mail indoors and for posting and did many messages for the staff, official and unofficial. We also looked after all visitors for the company. But shortly after the company moved office to 21 Dame Street, the roof fell in due to a marketing amalgamation with BP, and I became what is now called 'redundant' due to "rearrangement of our organisation through no fault of your own."

Arthur Henderson – Branch Manager

Tragedy at The Limerick Grand Prix 1936

There was also a famous race, which was held in Limerick, called the round-the-houses race. Shell had the contract for the supply of high-octane motor spirit at Roxboro Road Depot for all the entrants. In the race, the Duke of Grafton's vehicle went out of control during the race, hitting the Christian Brothers wall quite near to the Shell Depot. The victim was brought firstly to our depot before being transferred to Barrington's Hospital; he was very badly burned and sadly passed away during the night.

John 'Sean' McMahon, Lorry Boy and Driver

A Gentleman's job

It was a gentleman's job when I started 44 years ago (1938)...there was no staff association and management could give you the sack if they didn't like the look of your face. I earned 13s 5¹/₂d a week which would take you to the pictures on a Saturday.

Gordon Johnson (Recorded in 1982) – Head Office Administrator

By Air to America – *c.* 1937

Despatching the first newspapers to be sent by flying-boat from Foynes to America are (from left): Unknown, unknown, – Nestor (Irish Press Driver); Eddie McCarthy (Pan Am mechanic); Danny Cochrane (Irish Customs Officer); Padger Carney;Tom Crawford Young and Mickey Gilteran.

How I started in Shell

I was doing a line with Una, who was a sister-in-law of Jimmy Norton, and I went to the house this night, and he says to me, "By the way, how would you like to work in Shell? There's a job vacancy up there. Write in, tell them you have your Leaving Certificate." *Two days later, a letter from Shell arrives...*"Thank you for your letter of application but there's no vacancies". *The next night I was with Una again and Jimmy was there again and I was telling him this and he says that job is still open down there. I went out with Una and we came back that night and he says* "Give me a copy of that letter. I know what happened," *he says.* "What's that", *I says?* "You send in a new application with this address on it". *I sat down and wrote a new application. Got an interview the next day and a couple of days later got the job. 12a St. Anne's Mansions – they thought I was a gurrier. So it took me to put down a false address to get the job. So that's how I started in Shell.*

Harry Jordan – Internal Auditor

Amalgamating Shell and BP

Well, when I joined the company they had amalgamated in 1933 with BP and there were the Shell people and the BP people. The BP people apparently always had the good desks which came from BP and there was always that difference. "Oh, he's a BP man or he's a Shell man" *because it always seemed as if Shell took over BP and that BP didn't come out of the amalgamation as well as they should have. Harpur had come from Shell although Dixon was from BP. Harpur was very suitable to be a managing director He was a very popular MD and at his retirement speech, we all sang* "For he's a jolly good fellow".

Gordon Johnson – Head Office Administration

There were Characters!

It was more free and easy in those days. Everyone was mates. There were characters such as Joe Fay and John Lally and these fellas and in the morning they would be supposed to be coming in to get their orders for their deliveries – they were drivers – Joe Fahy would start tap-dancing in the hallway, Mick Smith would get up as well and they would dance around the hallway before they went out on deliveries.

Cecil Gillard – Dublin Terminal Administration

Ennis Depot

On the 4th of September 1939 (the day after World War II was declared), I had a visit from Inspector Tier from the Dublin Office who called and addressed me as follows: "McMahon, you are to report to the Ennis Depot in the morning to replace the Ennis Storekeeper". *(I later learned that this person had absconded with the day's cash takings and the Superintendent's car). In those days, it was a very common practice for Shell Management staff to address their subordinates by their surname only, a practice that reflected the social divide between white and blue-collar workers at that time.*

 My duties in Ennis commenced the following day and the company paid for my hotel

Bold Pioneering Experiments

Two pioneering experiments took place in 1938 in both of which Irish Shell played a key role. In the first of these (top photograph), a flying-boat over the Shannon was refuelled from a tanker-aircraft in mid-air before continuing on its journey. The scheme was devised to enable aircraft to take off with greater payloads. In the second experiment the Shorts flying Boat Maia *was specially modified to carry a smaller, swifter flying-boat on its back to operating height. Once in range of the pairs destination, the smaller flying-boat,* Mercury, *could separate and fly on to enable mails etc. to arrive in a shorter time. The bottom photograph shows the pair at Foynes before a flight to Montreal.*

expenses for a short period. At that time it was difficult to find accommodation and I was advised to contact Father Cahill, the local priest. He gave me the name and address of a landlady who was a widow woman. On arriving at the house and introducing myself to the landlady, I was asked if I drank or smoked? I was also informed that in this house the Rosary was recited every night at 10.30 pm. Having satisfied the landlady's questions, I took up full board and lodgings for the sum of 25 shillings a week for some years.

John 'Sean' McMahon, Lorry Boy and Driver

Working in the Garage

I went to work in the garage...the garage consisted of a tin shed, corrugated iron and the heating was two pipes which ran around the place...hygiene – out the window – you washed your hands and face at the tap out in the yard, cold water, no hot water, no towels, and the (piped) water was beginning to come into being at this time. Out in the back, there was another shed, a lean-to shed with paraffin oil...No power hoses.

Joe Coffey – Dublin MRC Administration

Maybe the Oil got in my blood...

I was working in Auto Services as a salesman at the time and I was standing on the forecourt on this evening. I had a bunch of notes in my hand as I had just sold a second-hand van when this car pulled up. It was a fella called Billy Tate. Now, Billy Tate was a rep with Shell at the time – he was the south city rep. I knew Billy and we got talking and Billy says to me, "By the way, Arthur, would you like a job back in Shell?" Jesus, this is heaven, I thought, I used to pray every night that I would get back to Shell, I loved the company and wanted to work for them. I don't know why, maybe the oil got into my blood and I had made so many friends there. "I can't do anything for you", he says, "except tell you that there's two vacancies on the junior sales staff and if I were you I'd send in an application without delay".

So, I applied, got an interview and was appointed to a job as a trainee representative and I went back to Shell in 1939 on my twenty-sixth birthday.

Arthur Henderson – Branch Manager

Superman

Tim Smith, motor inspector, who retired in 1967, told me another incident from the Foynes flying-boat days. The engine from a Shell tender boat had been overhauled at the Motor Repair Centre at Alexandra Road and was ready for return to Foynes. Mr Young was due at 10 am to inspect the engine before despatch. The mechanics had it running from 9.30 am in readiness of the visit when at five to ten the engine seized solid. Panic stations! Everything was tried but to no avail and then on the dot of ten, TACY (Crawford Young) drove into the yard. Tim's words "I got this burst of super strength and as I walked over to grab hold of the starting handle I knew something had to give. I spun the engine round and round and it started up...they were all slapping me on the back when he went."

Vincent Sheridan – Inspector Motor Mechanic

Serving Irish Aviation

(Top) A refuelling barge for the flying-boats at Foynes was designed by Tom Crawford Young and Mick Finnucane, the harbour pilot at Foynes. A converted ship's lifeboat, it was rebuilt at John Tyrrell's shipyard at Arklow.

(Bottom) An unusual vehicle used to refuel aircraft at Shannon and Collinstown airports in the late 1940s and 1950s was this three-wheeled tanker specially designed for airport work.

Filling the Ink Wells

I joined the company in 1938. The job consisted of filling ink wells on large long high desks with high stools, which I thought had gone out of use in Dickens' time; carrying cups of tea to the ladies only and posting letters.

Gordon Johnston – Head Office Administration

Chapter 4

The 1940s:
The 'Emergency'
and Shortages

The familiar gold cap badge worn by Shell drivers throughout the 1940s and on into the 1960s.

1940-1949 Petrol rationed – Private motoring ends during 'Emergency' – Belfast bombed – James Joyce dies – Central Bank established – Seán T O'Kelly becomes President – Atomic bombs dropped on Japan – World War 2 ends – Bread rationed in Dublin – Republic of Ireland established

Sean Lemass became Minister for Supplies on September 16th 1939 and on the same day introduced an Order covering the official rationing of petrol, to begin in October. (Two years later, Lemass also took over responsibility for Industry and Commerce, holding both portfolios until the Department of Supplies was wound up on July 21st 1945). The official allowance was 8 gallons a month for cars up to 10 hp; 12 gallons a month for cars 10 – 16 hp and a bit extra for doctors, vets, priests and commercial travellers. However, the Government announced that the value of each petrol coupon would vary according to the supply situation. As one retired Shell employee said, *"There still seemed to be plenty of petrol around, in fact there always seemed to be as much as you needed in those early days of the Emergency."*

No doubt, the early ease of supplies was due to the stockpiling that the oil companies had been undertaking for some time as they filled garage tanks to the brim with a view to gaining as much storage space for product at their own storage installations. The situation was soon to change. The vast bulk of Ireland's petrol supplies came through Britain and these were abruptly cut to a mere trickle at the end of 1939. As a result the promised ration was cancelled and supplies became increasingly hard to obtain.

A Combined Delivery System was agreed between the Government and the Oil companies and this was set-up with a view to eliminating any wastage of scarce resources. At the same time the Government introduced a Maximum Prices Order (which was to endure until late in 1949). The Combined Delivery System remained in place until January 1st 1949, at which time the oil companies were allowed to import and sell as much oil as they wished. But despite the ending of 'The Emergency' in 1945, rationing officially remained in force for a further six years before finally coming to an end on December 17th 1951.

During this period, supplies were also extended from an unlikely source. Between 1936 and 1938, five alcohol factories were built and managed by the Semi-State company Ceimici Teoranta. The factories were located at Carndonagh and Labbaisish in County Donegal, Ballina in County Mayo, Carrickmacross in County Monaghan and Cooley in County Louth. The primary purpose behind the venture was to find an alternative use for a huge surplus potato crop in these areas. The Government obliged the oil companies to purchase the output of these factories and to transport it by rail and road to, in Irish Shell's case, Alexandra Road, for blending with motor spirit. During the Emergency years the alcohol helped to stretch the meagre supplies of petrol. However, never happy with this arrangement, when production finally ceased in the early 1950s, the oil companies were somewhat relieved as the 'landed' cost of industrial alcohol at Dublin was approximately three times the cost of imported motor spirit.

For Irish Shell, at first, not much changed in the early days of the 'Emergency' apart from air-raid drills and the provision of gas masks to all Shell employees. In a photograph that appeared widely in the press, the Shell Managing Director, Captain Harpur, was photographed among a group demonstrating the correct wearing of a gas mask during a drill at the company's Alexandra Road terminal. Understandably, there was a tremendous amount of anxiety amongst staff regarding their jobs, but Captain Harpur travelled the country addressing staff at the different installations and depots and assuring them that their employment was safe. This was a

'The Emergency'

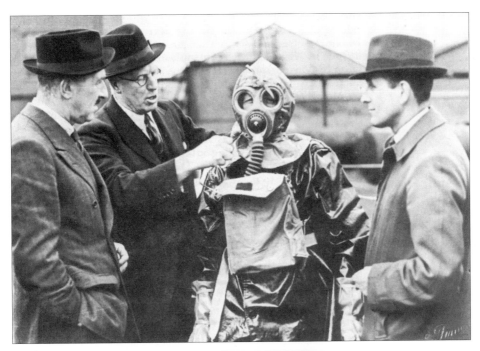

The photograph (top) shows Captain Hugh St.G Harpur, (on left) Managing Director of Irish Shell Limited, looking at a gas mask and protective clothing during an Air Raid Precaution practice drill at the company's Alexandra Road installation in May 1939, just prior to the outbreak of World War II. Petrol supplies for private motoring soon ran out as 'The Emergency' progressed. A few motorists converted their cars (bottom photograph) to run on town gas, which was stored in a rubberised tank on the roof. However, supplies of the coal needed for the manufacture of the gas soon came to an end as well, and these cars too, were laid-up for the duration.

major commitment by the company and was greatly appreciated by all those who served during this difficult period. Inevitably, it led to a number of unsatisfactory situations. One was with regard to drivers, for as supplies of product dwindled, the company decided to man their lorries and tankers with two drivers rather than have men idle who were no longer strictly necessary. At the end of 'The Emergency' when the company tried to revert to the original manning levels, the unions insisted on each driver retaining a helper on the basis of the precedent established during these years. This practice was to remain contentious and continued until the sixties before finally coming to an end. While staff retained their jobs, many chose to join either the Free State Defence Forces or the British Army, and those that did so were not replaced.

What petrol there was was distributed during this period by a 'Pool Board' under a 'no-brand name' basis. Brand names were removed from the top of petrol pumps and all the oil companies brought their control systems together a a single location at Alexandra Road, Dublin. The delivery lorries of Shell & BP, Esso, Caltex and McMullens, all operated with two drivers from separate companies and the system was intended to provide equal treatment for all customers. (It was not until 1946 that branded petrol pumps returned and 1948 before branded products returned).

Two Shell employees who remembered theses times were Oliver Talbot and Gordon Johnston. Oliver Talbot, a Depot Supervisor at this time recalls some of the difficulties that arose between the oil companies at this time:

During the 'Emergency' supplies dwindled and the Oil companies amalgamated their transport and each vehicle had a driver and co-driver of different companies. When coupons were introduced, meetings were held every morning and coupons were counted. The customers' orders of all companies were then routed for delivery and of course, there was a bit of in-fighting, each representative making sure that his customers were given priority in deliveries.

One of the most aggravating things during the 'Emergency' was that we had a very small quota, especially for kero, and we had to hand over our customers to Esso nearly every month, they being an American company, they received bigger supplies.

Gordon Johnson recalled the unloved 'coupons':

All products were rationed, therefore deliveries were recorded against each customer on cards 12"X 8" approx. filed in large boxes. Petrol deliveries were

Defending the Free State

At the start of the 'Emergency', the Irish Army Air Corps had a total of around sixty aircraft to defend the Free State's airspace. Avro Ansons (top) were used for coastal patrol while these Hawker Hurricanes (bottom) were the first line of fighter defence. Fuel shortages throughout the 'Emergency' were a very severe constraint on the activities of the Air Corps.

checked against coupons, these coupons were then taken to Griffith Barracks for destruction.

Petrol for private cars became increasingly unavailable by the middle of 1941 and as a consequence, the money brought in by road taxes into the Exchequer dropped accordingly. As a result, spending on roads was at first curtailed and by 1941 had stopped altogether. The inevitable end came about when supplies of petrol for private motoring ceased altogether at the end of March 1942. In an attempt to compensate for the loss of private transport, the Government amended the Road Traffic Acts, increasing the numbers permitted to be carried in buses, and allowing the law to come down heavier on bicycle theft. Vehicle speed limits were reduced to save wear and tear on tyres, and in Dublin, public transport ceased altogether after 9 pm.

As one can imagine, people's lives were severely affected by these changes as rationing and petrol shortages began to take hold. Petrol availability became a major problem for many from an early stage and public transport almost ceased. The humble bicycle underwent a revival and came to be worth its weight in gold. At the same time there was a small increase in horse-drawn traffic and for a period, a small number of motorists converted their cars to run on gas stored in large bags on their roof. Such cars were not put off the road, but they received no supplies of petrol or tyres and no guarantee of supplies of fuel for making the gas. And as coal supplies also dwindled, there was a gradual and then a quick deterioration of all rail services. From April 1944, the petrol ration, tiny as it was, that was still supplied to doctors and clergymen living in the city was withdrawn altogether. Also, in the same year, a new Transport Act was introduced to bring about the amalgamation of Great Southern Railways and the Dublin United Tramway Company into Córas Iompair Eireann (CIE), a national transport company. One form of transport that came into its own again during this time was that using the canals and in 1942, twenty-nine new barges were ordered to be used for the transportation of turf, while Alexandra Quay, adjacent to the Shell terminal, was used for the storage of coal and turf reserves for the duration of 'The Emergency'.

As 'The Emergency' continued into its third year, things improved to a certain extent, and Britain released enough fuel to meet the country's essential needs. Nevertheless, by the time 'The Emergency' ended in the Irish Free State, its industrial production had fallen by some 30 per cent, while agricultural production was also severely affected by the misfortune of

Plenty in the midst of Scarcity

Wrapping up after a successful Dublin Spring Show, John Lally relaxes for the camera, letting water spill out of an oil barrel.

Calibration of the vehicle tanks was laboriously carried out by lifting up 5 gallon measures of water to the fill point, while the sergeant of Weights and Measures carefully marked the dip rod, step by step. Paddy Mulvey, on one occasion in the 1940s, after the job had been soberly completed to official satisfaction, couldn't resist the urge to liven up an otherwise unexciting time and place, and finding himself with a full tank of water for disposal, he opened the taps and drove through the town of Carrick-on-Shannon!

a series of bad harvests. Not surprisingly, there were record unemployment rates of 62,000 men and 8,000 women and the number of people emigrating reached 40,000 for the year 1948.

The decade had begun with Foynes at the forefront of the aviation world and as the conflict continued, Foyne's position as a refuelling base continued to be of critical importance with regard to the movement of aircraft across the Atlantic. Meanwhile, the construction of the new airport and the runways required for land-based aircraft continued apace and Rineanna came into use during 1945. At first, passengers crossing the Atlantic disembarked at Foynes and travelled by road to Rineanna for onward connections by land-planes, but as the added impetus given to aircraft development as a result of the conflict continued, so the importance of Foynes declined and that of Rineanna, increasingly simply called Shannon, grew. Shell established its presence at the new airport right from the start and continued to be a key provider of fuels and lubricants to the trans-Atlantic and other traffic using the new airport.

Stanley Russell, who served at the Foynes base and at Shannon Airport recalls:

I went to Foynes in November 1942 as assistant to Brendan O'Reilly. Michael Cox was the cox in charge of boats. There were two boats with tanks and pumping equipment for the fuels used by the flying boats that landed and took off from Foynes. The boats were 'SHELLEIRE' (1,200 gallons capacity) and 'SHELLAVIA' (1,000 gallons capacity). The fuel was stored at the Foynes installation which in turn was supplied by coastal tankers from the UK. Fuel was delivered by motor tanker from the Foynes installation to the boats at Foynes pier.

The Flying boats were tied to their moorings in the Estuary between Foynes Island and Foynes Harbour. All the passengers arriving on flying boats were transferred by road from Foynes to Shannon and then taken by British Airways land-planes to Southampton.

Shell also had a storage tank and refuelling truck at Shannon Airport and Eric Paton was the man in charge there. Transatlantic land planes took over in 1945, so Shannon Airport (Rineanna) was our base from then on. Bigger storage tanks were installed with all the equipment required.

In 1948 an era came to an end with the retirement of Captain Hugh St. G Harpur. Captain Harpur had served Shell for twenty-six years and had been Managing Director for eighteen of those years, a period longer than any

Fishing and Golfing ...

A SIDELIGHT
ON
RISH SHELL
1948

Upon his retirement in 1948, the popular Captain Harpur was presented with this fine caricature showing him pursuing his two favourite past-times, Fishing and Golfing.

other managing director of the company, before or since. A colourful and flamboyant character, he had generated great loyalty amongst staff who were genuinely sorry to see him leave. He was widely regarded as a 'character', a title no doubt enhanced by his favourite drinking companions – the famous R M Smyllie, Editor of *The Irish Times* and the writer Brian O'Nolan, who wrote under the pseudonym of Myles na gCopaleen. Captain Harpur would meet 'Smyllie ' and Myles in The Palace Bar, or 'Indignation House' as it was called by the staff of *The Irish Times*. His replacement was Tom Crawford Young who had originally joined Shell-Mex in London in 1930, moving to Ireland three years later as motor supervisor for Irish Shell. In 1945 he was appointed Manager and a year later General Manager.

At Captain Harpur's farewell dinner, he was presented with a framed caricature showing him pursuing his two favourite past-times – golfing and fishing, and staff sang *"For he's a jolly good fellow"*. Sadly, he was to have little opportunity to enjoy his retirement, being claimed by cancer just three years later.

Tom Crawford Young

Tom Crawford Young, ('TACY' to many, but not in his hearing!) became Managing Director of Irish Shell and BP in 1948 in succession to Captain Hugh St. G Harpur. Over the next sixteen years he was responsible for many far-reaching changes and while often regarded as a stern man, he gained the respect of all for his even-handiness and integrity.

Shell Voices

Even if we're a bit slack from time to time...

When World War II broke out, Hugh Harpur addressed staff around the country and told them that their jobs would be safe for the duration of hostilities:

If Mr Harpur said that, you know, we would put our absolute life in his hands. Mr Harpur said "It doesn't matter if we're a bit slack from time to time, you'll all be kept." That was appreciated because there was a lot of married men there who were worried about their future with the company if things collapsed, because in the 1930s when I joined the Shell company it was very hard to get a job and you were thankful to have one. The staff were reduced by members leaving to join the Irish and British forces.

Gordon Johnston – Head Office Administration

Tragedy

In the early 1940s, Tom Crawford Young's only son died of meningitis, an event which greatly affected everybody in the company:

When Crawford Young's only son died, that was the saddest thing ever in the company, and indeed, Mr Harpur wrote a note on the notice board to say that we weren't to mention the death of his son to Mr Young when he came back. It was a terrible blow to him and even to the day he died, he and his wife never got over the death of their son from meningitis. From then on he changed and threw himself into the company in a way he hadn't before.

Paddy Anthony – Retail Representative

The Shell 'Huckster' Shop

As you can imagine the pace of life was much easier than modern times. Remembering the old kero trucks with their 500 gallon tanks doing the rounds of the countryside making deliveries of 5 and 10 gallons of kerosene. On one occasion a kero truck happened to be in the Depot and the motor inspector arrived in and immediately put on his warehouse coat and proceeded to carry out an inspection. One of the things he remarked on was the cleanliness of the toolbox at the back of the cab while the tools were in the cab. The driver, Joe Lane, had a 'huckster' shop and used the toolbox to bring the cans and jars of sweets, etc., for sale to the kero customers on his route. The motor Inspector was T A C Young, later Managing Director.

Oliver Talbot – Depot Supervisor

Senator T V Honan

My superintendent in Ennis at that time was Senator T V Honan. The Senator was a lover of flowers and on his instigation, we planted gladiola bulbs from Powers of Waterford in the grass area surrounding the office. In time, we developed a very commendable floral display in this area. As it happened, one day the Horticulture Inspector came to the office and admired our work, so impressed was he that he also made a call to T V Honan's house to pass on his compliments. Unfortunately, one week later on arriving back in Ennis, having

Outings ...

Head Office staff pictured during an outing to Brittas Bay around 1950 and below, tennis at Malahide in September 1948.

been home to Limerick for the weekend, I was shocked to see that our floral project had been completely vandalised. The 'Super', on making his usual visit to my office observed what had happened and being a lover of flowers was naturally very upset. He commented "If only I had the thugs that caused this damage, I would have them behind bars". He returned with a sign displaying 'Trespassers will be prosecuted'. It just goes to show that vandalism was also part of our society back in the 1940s.

In the Ennis Depot at that time there was no electricity and the office was lit with the aid of a kerosene lamp. We had two 30' X 9' tanks, and having no electricity, all supplies had to be pumped to the lorries by semi-rotary pumps.

Ennis had many attractions for me in those days, on weekends, we would sometimes travel to Lahinch or Kilkee on the old West Clare Railway. I was a member of the LDF Field Ambulance Section and had many a laugh while on manoeuvres with that organisation. Then, we also had our local cinema. On one occasion, having left my bicycle outside the cinema, there was an urgent call by the LDF to commandeer all kinds of transport. When I came out of the cinema that evening, there was no sign of my bicycle. I didn't get it back until the next day.

John 'Sean' McMahon, Lorry Boy and Driver

All Night Fire Watching – Men Only

During this period, known as the 'Emergency', one of the jobs was to carry the MD's bicycle to the hall. The office was on the first floor on the corner of George's Street and Dame Street. It was over a gentlemen's outfitters called Burtons.

Air raid drill consisted of a rush to the basement at the sound of a whistle. All-night fire watching was practised on occasions from Friday night until Saturday morning by four people – men only. Heavy black-out curtains were placed on all windows.

Gordon Johnston – Head Office Administration

Joining the Board

In 1945 I had been demobbed by the British Army, and returned home to Spiddal. On a visit to London, I went to my Club and sat with Mr George Wilson who was a high executive of Shell-Mex and BP. I must admit I didn't know his profession at the time although I did know he was very interested in fishing and bridge! He was very noticeable because of the bright red colour of his face. At that time I was giving up any idea I might have had of returning to London to work as it had always been my ambition to remain at home and I told him this. He then asked if I was interested in joining the Board of Irish Shell. Most things in my life have just happened and have never been planned. I said "Yes" and on Wednesday 18th December 1946, I was co-opted to the Board and attended my first Board meeting at 21 Dame Street on 14th March the following year. My original director's fee was £100 per annum!

Lord Killanin (Recorded in 1984) – Director

Flights of Memory

'Flights of Memory' was the appropriate title of a small booklet (shown at top) published by Irish Shell in 1956 to commemorate the role it had played in the development of aviation. Several of the photographs appearing in the booklet are reproduced elsewhere in this book – in particular with regard to flying-boat operations at Foynes. The centre photograph shows several enthusiastic amateurs – all members of the Irish Aero Club with their first aircraft, a DH Moth, at Baldonnel in 1928. The figure on the right of the photograph is Captain Harpur who became managing director of Irish Shell two years later. The others are – from left; R N Mitchell, Captain F Crossley; C E Mitchell; C E McConnell; Colonel J Fitzmaurice and Mr Reddy.

The bottom photograph shows a rare visitor to Dublin Airport in 1955 – a Royal Air Force Gloster Meteor being refuelled by Shell-BP.

After the 'Emergency'

Private cars which were stored during the War (the 'Emergency' to us) gradually came back onto the road. Petrol rationing continued and only 'pool' petrol was available. This was of low quality and only suitable for low compression engines. It had a propensity to 'pink' causing a sharp pinging noise from the engine and inadequate power. Most cars were eight or ten horse power (RAC rating) and the annual road tax was £1 per horsepower. The cost of a driving licence was ten shillings (50p) and the only requirement was that you had to be over sixteen years of age. Woodbine cigarettes were sold in lots of five in a close fitting paper bag and a box of matches was 1^1/$_2$ d.

On my first visit to Dublin in 1946, there were large ricks of turf all along the main road in the Phoenix Park, emergency supplies, and there were air raid shelters in O'Connell Street. At the end of 1947, I started my apprenticeship at G A Brittan's Service Department in Ringsend Road. Next door was the CIE garage where numerous Leyland Titan buses were based, mostly ZA or ZC registrations and all with their starting handles sticking out in front. Guinness had a fleet of Vulcan lorries, the Irish Glass Bottle Company had Thornycrofts, Boland's Bakery had Austins. All of these and other makes are now history.

Vincent Sheridan – Inspector Motor Mechanic

Head Office Junior Mailing Boy

I joined the company in 1948. I started in the Mailing Department. The company head office where I worked was situated at 21 Dame Street, over Burtons tailors. To this day, the name 'Burtons' is still carved in stone on the building.

Although the Second World War had been over three years, there still remained a spill-over of customs and practices which the company had adopted duering the 'Emergency'. Envelopes were recycled. Incoming envelopes were opened carefully and graded for re-use by sealing them with labels. Post for places within reasonable walking distance of the office, such as Capel Street, Westmoreland Street, O'Connell Street (Esso and Caltex), Westland Row, Camden Street, City Hall and Dublin Castle, were delivered by hand by the junior mailing boy.

Many of the staff had bicycles and quite often, staff arriving just in time to catch the time books would just throw their bicycles against the railings at the rear of the building. The junior mailing boy was expected to put these bicycles in the basement, either by carrying them down a steep stairs or by wheeling them down a slipway whilst running down the steps beside it. Brakes were usually scarce and one had to be fairly athletic to keep up with the runaway steed. This job was only done after the time books had been removed at 9.05 am and replaced by a late book on the mailing department counter. This book was supervised by the senior mailing official, Joe Delahoyde. Joe was middle-aged, had a red complexion and sleek Brylcreamed hair, and was very exact. Four lates in a month led to a reprimand by your boss and a penalty of having to work an extra Saturday or two. (It was normal at the time to work 9 to 12.30 one Saturday in seven). Some of the rosters required head office staff to go to Dublin Installation at Alexandra Road to take customer orders. Preceding my first appearance there, I rang Harry Jordan to whom I would report, to find out the route I should take (on my bike) to get to the FOB site office. Harry gave me the information, warned about getting my wheels stuck in the train tracks on Alexandra Road, and finally

Staff Outing

Shell staff photographed at Portmarnock Golf Club during their annual outing in 1954.
From left: Gerry Mackey, Bertie McLeod, Angela Rice, Pat Walsh, Terry O'Neill, Mrs Dorothy Gillett, Ray Gillett,
John Douglas, Joe Whitten, Mrs Doreen Marsland, May Brady, Ken Wall, Bill Taaffe, Ann Keane, Mrs Maguire,
Mrs Fred Dixon, Gordon Johnson, Bill Murray, Breffni O'Rourke, Kevin Maguire, Walter Joyce, Mrs Alma Reid,
Jack Andrews, Eileen Pappin, Angela O'Flanagan, Sam Pullen, Mrs Joyce, Norman Pappin, Marie Nicholson,
Mick O'Connell, Mrs Fitzell, Crea McGaley, T A Crawford Young, Albert Fitzell, Una Murray, Paddy Kavanagh,
Mrs Swendell, Ivan Marsland, Mrs Young, John (Blue) Byrne, Statia McEntaggart, Ned Swendell, Val Long,
Michael Bannon, Jimmy Cosgrave, Eric Welsh, Peg Long, Mrs Pratt, Eithne Groves, Eithne Murphy, Des Groves,
Joe Pratt, Terry Barr, Patricia Purcell, Bill Aston, John Colfor, Tom Loughman, John Colfor, Dolores Hackett,
Gerry Ryan, Tom Maher, Jack Dunne, Clare Dumbleton, Jimmy Norton, Liam McCabe, Dick Sinnott, Celia Dunne,
Ethel Breen, Cicely McCabe, Mrs Doyle, Nancy Mulligan, Sidney Hart, Mervyn Doyle and Shelia Garvey.

charged me not to arrive without "the cigar and the sweets". On Saturday, I arrived with both, and Harry, to overcome his embarrassment, opened up the sweet bag, peered in and said "Where's the Peggy's Leg?"

Paddy Kavanagh – Senior Personnel Assistant

Tie-line Terrors
Well, I joined in 1948 down in Dublin Terminal as office boy... one of my responsibilities was the switchboard which was one of those upright switchboards with all the holes and you put the plugs in, all manual, and if you wanted to speak to anybody in Head Office there was a 'tie-line' and you plugged into the tie-line and dialled it up by turning a handle which rung a bell at the Head Office switchboard where there was a lady and she would come through the phone – she might has well have come through in person – and she would lift you out of it and you know it was just very difficult to get it right – you either rang too long or not long enough! If you didn't ring enough she wouldn't answer and if you rang too much she would come through the phone at you. And anybody who wanted to make a call had to make it through the switchboard, nobody had their own phone, they were all just extensions off the switchboard.

Des Murphy – Personnel Manager

"That man is a nun"
Mrs Hanley, the (Head Office) Tea lady, requisitioned the Junior Mailing Boy to help her hand out refreshment to staff at their desks. She had names and descriptions for staff, such as "the boy with the golden hair" – Gordon Johnson – or the "man with the hearing-aid" – Charlie Stephens – or "that man is a nun" – Teddy Heuston – meaning he took no sugar.

Paddy Kavanagh – Senior Personnel Assistant

Fred Dixon
Fred Dixon was a great character. Harpur once told Fred Dixon to go down and sack a driver in Fermoy and Dixon when down and he changed his mind and gave him another chance. He told Harpur what he had decided and Harpur said if it's alright with you then it's alright with me. The man died shortly afterwards and Dixon was always delighted that he didn't sack him. After he died his widow got a pension for years and years so Dixon was never keen to sack anybody. It wasn't in his nature anyway.

Gordon Johnston – Head Office Administration

The long lunch hour
Petrol was still on ration in 1948 and used coupons had to be brought to Griffith Barracks each day. I had to cycle there several times, but generally at about 11.00 am each day, Joe Delahoyd would put on his coat and disappear with the bundle under his arm. It was only after a long time that I found out that Joe lived somewhere near the barracks which was on the South Circular Road and was enjoying a long lunch hour.

Paddy Kavanagh – Senior Personnel Assistant

Shell Drivers at Nenagh – 1948

Shell drivers John 'Sean' McMahon, Sean Butler and Joe Slattery photographed (top) at Nenagh in 1948. The second photograph, which has been hand-tinted, shows John 'Sean' McMahon with his Shell Delivery Lorry.

The new Set

I joined in 1949... a lot of us joined around that period, we were part of the new set and of course, at that stage, when we came in, I suppose we were all dead scared on our first day. It was like going into secondary school from primary school but when we got there the existing chaps that were there, much older, long service, they made us very welcome. There was a great mixture of young and not-so-young and that mixture existed right up to the day I left. When I was old, the young boys and girls in the office mixed very well and everybody was on first name terms – there was a good atmosphere.

Alfie Duff – Engineering Assistant

The Shell Productivity Scheme

Due to the fact that my mother was ill, I requested a transfer back to Limerick. My request was eventually granted in 1943 and I returned to Limerick taking up the position of Lorry Driver. I was given a new lorry, which was a special Shell Aviation Service lorry supplying to Shannon Airport and to the Military who had an Avro Anson based there.

Big changes took place upon the introduction of the Shell Productivity Scheme. S/R hand-operated pumps were done away with and sophisticated pumps introduced. During this time, each delivery vehicle was taken off the road for calibration by an inspector of Weights & Measures.

John 'Sean' McMahon, Lorry Boy and Driver

"The Chain Gang"

The second floor (of Head Office) was full of activity. It housed what was known as the "Chain Gang", who sat on high stools at Victorian desks, with brass bars on top. The "Chain Gang" contained most of the characters in the building. Upon the entry of Mrs Hanley onto that floor, one might hear one person say to another "Are you fo'coffee?"

Paddy Kavanagh – Senior Personnel Assistant

"Be consistent in your Inconsistencies"

I joined in May 1949 in Dame Street just as the 'Emergency' petrol rationing was lifted. After a year or so manually transferring sales from tickets onto customer record cards, the company set up a General Ledgers and Costs section where I found myself with Tom O'Carroll and Ned O'Leary under Jock McColl, Chief Accountant – he of "I have been watching those Corporation workmen for the past hour and they haven't lifted a shovel" *fame. We had regular visits from a Mr Callendar from Shell-Mex House and I have never forgotten his favourite edict* "Be consistent in your inconsistencies". *Down through the years it was evidently the ambition of Shell-Mex personnel to visit Irish Shell on whatever pretext. I do believe Guinness must take some of the blame!*

Paddy Foley – Retail Services Manager

The *Shellfoil*

Before the fuel oil site was built there was a boat moored down in Alexandra Basin called the Shellfoil and it had a Scottish captain called Doughal McDonald who lived on the boat

Golden Age Goalkeeper

The late 1940s and 1950s were a golden age of Soccer in Ireland and Christy O'Callaghan, an operative at Dublin terminal, was at the heart of the action as goal-keeper for the brilliant Shamrock Rovers team. In a career that spanned nine years at the top level – Christy, pictured here in action – won three FAI Cup medals, two Leinster Cup medals, four Shield Trophies, two President's Cup Trophies and one League Championship.

and that was where they used to store fuel oil – on the boat – before this fuel oil/bitumen site was built.

Des Murphy – Personnel Manager

During World War II, none of the oil companies had sufficient fuel oil storage and a facility came about in an unusual way. Originally owned by a Dutch company, an oil tanker called The Danmark was going about its business during the war in waters off Scotland. Hitler thought he'd brighten things up so he blew the stern off it. It was towed to port in Scotland where a couple of gun turrets were put on it, they cut the stern off, plated it up and sealed it off and it was used as a storage tank for refuelling various visiting warships. Later, at the end of its use in the UK, (now renamed the Shellfoil*), it was towed into Dublin. One or two of The Danmark's original pumps were still there and there was a great big compartment for stowing barrelled lubricating oil so three small boilers were put into it which fed the main pump. Fuel oil was pumped into Shell and then underground into the Irish American Oil Company. There had been a log recording the various visiting warships which had signed for their fuel during its time in the UK. Sadly, this log no longer exists as it would have made interesting reading so many years later.*

Leo O'Carroll – Manager, Dublin Terminal

The Shellfoil

Before the fuel oil site was built at Dublin Terminal, a boat called the Shellfoil was moored at Alexandra Basin on which fuel oil was stored. The Shellfoil, familar to all those who worked at Dublin Terminal in the 1950s, had a Scottish captain called Doughal McDonald who lived on the boat.

Dublin Terminal Faces

Joseph Donnellan (far left) was the first laboratory Assistant at Dublin Terminal. The laboratory was then situated at the end wall of the Terminal and was a rather primitive affair of corrugated iron with a cement floor and no heating.
The second photograph shows Tommy Ryan (left) and Des Murphy photographed in 1949 in the Dublin Terminal Office.

101

Chapter 5

The 1950s:
Enter the Distributors

The Aladdin Pink Paraffin sign was a familiar sight right through the 1950s and into the 1960s.

1950-1959 Last trams replaced by buses – Abbey Theatre burned down – Insurance Inquiry – Record tourism – An Tóstal Festival – Bord Fáilte established – Ireland joins the United Nations – Suez crisis – Ronnie Delaney wins Gold at Melbourne Olympics – Seán Lemass becomes Taoiseach – Treaty of Rome

Tom Crawford Young's arrival as Managing Director in 1948 ushered in changed times for the company. The post-Emergency years were a peculiar mixture of continuing shortages and significant change in Ireland. Undoubtedly, there was a sense of the country having been successfully steered through a period of great danger and a new, if somewhat fragile, business confidence was abroad. In the late forties and early fifties, Shell had two significant advantages over its competitors. The first was the word 'Irish' in its name. Secondly, many people had fathers or brothers or sisters in the British Army during the war. Shell had been part of the Commonwealth, whereas Esso and Caltex were regarded as foreigners. While Esso was particularly strong in the area of its motor spirit business, Irish Shell's strength lay in its commercial sales.

The significance of Shannon Airport and its successful demonstration of what could be achieved by native enterprise at this crucial time cannot be over-estimated and the knowledge that Irish Shell had played a key role in all of the developments at Shannon, and Foynes, served to give the company an added status. While the country continued to haemorrhage through the twin wounds of unemployment and emigration, the realisation grew that self-help was the only real solution and that whatever our difficulties, there were opportunities to be grasped and acted upon.

One such opportunity was perceived by Irish Shell, as, with the advent of the 1950s, came a greatly increased awareness by the State of the economic importance of good roads in attracting much-needed industry to Ireland. The result was a much increased capital expenditure on the roads. As a result of this new policy Irish Shell constructed the first bulk bitumen plant in the world not attached to a refinery. Prior to 1952, the company handled all its bitumen in drums, five of them to a ton. Its decision to set up a sophisticated new plant to handle bulk bitumen was unusual, but it had been made possible by technical developments in trans-shipment from the Caribbean (all bitumen shipments to Irish Shell coming from Shell's plant on the island of Curaçao off the coast of Venezuela) and by the Government's decision to spend £500,000 on its road building plan. Prior to this development, the roads of the Republic had been notoriously dusty and with eighteen miles of road to every thousand of the population (compared to England's four) the cost of the surfacing was a key factor in the Government's roads budget. Bitumen travelled to Ireland aboard three tankers, the mv *Pallium*, the mv *Pagiola* and the mv *Petula* to supply the new plant which turned out to be a tremendous commercial success for Irish Shell enabling it to supply bitumen at a cost considerably cheaper than had been possible before its construction. Shell's position in the Irish bitumen market was dominant during this time and as well as supplying the 26 county market, Irish Shell also supplied the Northern Ireland market.

John Buggle, who worked in this area, recalled the growth of the bitumen business during this time:

> The biggest customers for bitumen were the Government, and Roadstone were also enormous. In fact, Roadstone bought more bitumen than all the County Councils combined, around 90,000 tons if my memory served me correctly. The bitumen business grew very quickly during the 1950s. It was run here by an agent, McCreath Taylors, who were a Scottish firm and who also distributed for Shell-Mex and BP in Scotland and Northern Ireland. Eventually, Irish Shell decided to end this arrangement around about 1969 and took over the business themselves.

Dublin Installation – 1950's

Dublin Installation was first established at the end of 1908 when the Asiatic Petroleum Company purchased the site. Our top photograph shows tankers refuelling from the overhead gantry in 1954/5 and a general view of the site taken in 1958 for inclusion in the 'Book of the Year' publication by Irish Shell.

The inaugural issue of the first Irish Shell staff magazine in July 1953 recorded activity at the bitumen site rather wistfully:

> *Visitors who were present at the opening ceremony of this site would be amazed at the scene of activity it presents today. Hardly a minute goes by without a vehicle pulling in to be loaded with fuel oil or bitumen. At the same time, as fast as a gang of men are filling barrels with various grades of Bitumen, so are they being conveyed and loaded on to Rail Wagons by fork lift trucks. These in turn are whisked away by our own Diesel Engine. We wonder how long it will be before a Station Master is installed.*

In 1954, a hugely significant change in the way that Irish Shell did business occurred when it decided to adopt the Authorised Distributor (AD) policy which had been introduced in the UK the previous year. Reflecting the high proportion of tractor business enjoyed by the company, many of the new distributors appointed by the company were already active in tractor sales. Over the years, many of the Authorised Distributors that were established have come and gone or evolved through several changes of ownership, while a small number have continued from their establishment in the 1950s in business down to current times.

The first of the Irish Authorised Distributors was Inishowen Oil Company, founded in 1953 by Charles Kelly. The company continues to this day and is owned and operated by his sons, Seamus and Sean, whose own sons, Conor and Mark, are also involved in the business. In a similar vein, Donegal Oil became an Authorised Distributor in July 1954 and is now run by Arthur McMahon, grandson of the founder, also Arthur McMahon. Kerry Petroleum, founded in October 1954 by Frank Blennerhassett, is now run by his son, Roland. Of the other original Authorised Distributors, Leinster Petroleum, South of Ireland Petroleum, Vale Oil and Oriel Oil are still in operation but no longer under the ownership of their founders. The remainder have either disbanded, changed or amalgamated, and are now represented in the network by Capital Oil, Corrib Oil, Glen Fuels, Shannonside Oil, Midland Oil and LMS.

The year 1956 saw the advent of the Suez Crisis at a time when the Republic's dependence on oil was strikingly shown in an OEEC survey, which estimated consumption of petroleum as an element in energy needs, and which found that it counted for 39% in the Republic as against 13-14% in the United Kingdom. As things turned out, the Suez crisis did not escalate into a major difficulty at the pumps of Irish filling stations, and supplies

Early Days at Inishowen Oil

Top: Charles Kelly (on left) the founder of Inishowen Oil, pictured circa 1960 with Joe Doherty and two of the company's early tankers.

Above left: The arrival of the bulk storage tanks for Inishowen Oil Company Depot in Carndonagh in 1954.

Above right: (from left) – back row: Eddie 'Jack' Doherty, Charlie Hegarty, Bobby Carey, Charles Kelly, Reggie McGonagle. Front row: Jimmy Doherty, Seamus Kelly, Sean Duddy and Sean Kelly.

Left: Charles Kelly (left) with the first petrol pump in Carndonagh shortly after the establishment of Inishowen Oil in 1954. Local shopkeeper Joe Toye is pictured on the right.

soon returned to normal levels. Also, in June 1956, the legendary RAF flying ace, Douglas Bader, visited Ireland for the Aero Club of Ireland's Air Display at Weston aerodrome. A Shell employee, Douglas Bader was in charge of Shell's extensive aircraft fleet. Bader flew to Dublin for the occasion with his wife, Thelma, in his Shell company aircraft, a twin-engined Miles Gemini. During his visit he played a round of golf at Dublin's Grange Golf Club with Freddie Dixon, impressing enormously with his golfing ability and forceful personality.

In November 1957, the first stock of BP Domesticol was laid down at Dublin Installation. This marked a significant 'first' for Irish Shell, and BP Domesticol, which was introduced especially to suit the needs of small domestic boilers, proved a great success on the Irish market. Coupled with the long-established Shell Domestic Fuel Oil, this new fuel allowed oil to become a practical and economic proposition for the average householder. To help develop this market further, the company showed a wide range of oil-fired units at exhibitions in Cork, Sligo and the Royal Dublin Society's Spring Show.

Other developments at this time included the opening of a new installation at Cork and the introduction of the Hydrant Refuelling System at Shannon Airport. The new Cork Installation was officially opened by the Lord Mayor of Cork on the October 8th 1957. The new installation had been three years in construction and set new standards for its advanced design as well as providing first-class working conditions for the staff. Prior to 1950 the old depot at Marina Road had not handled anything heavier than gas oil. In that year, a site was purchased at Centre Park Road, and the official opening in 1957 was the culmination of a long process of planning and construction at the Cork site.

A Hydrant Refuelling System was introduced by Shell at Shannon in 1956 and was designed to solve the problem caused by Shannon's status as a 'stop-over' airport, whereby aircraft were required to be refuelled while on the ground for only a relatively short time. Prior to the system being introduced, this had led to congestion of vehicles and aircraft on the tarmac. The introduction of a system of pipes and hydrant points at each of the aircraft 'stands' allowed fuel to be always 'on tap' and did away with the need for tanker vehicles having to return to their base to refuel.

The Shell exhibition of oil paintings, on world tour, arrived in Ireland early in 1958 and was shown at the Cork Ideal Homes Exhibition, where it was seen by between fifty and sixty thousand people. Subsequently, the exhibition was on view in the Royal Hibernian Hotel, Dublin, for a short

Douglas Bader Visits

In 1956, the legendary RAF Air Ace, Douglas Bader, visited Dublin with his wife Thelma, to attend the Air Display of the Aero Club of Ireland at Weston. Bader, who was a Shell employee is pictured signing autographs and (below) with J V Tighe (on left) and Freddie Dixon at Weston.

period in the early part of the summer, where again it attracted a great deal of interest.

At this time, the company also had a very active Social and Sports Club based at its Head Office. Its boating section was the proud owner of a motor boat 'Aileen', which was used for cruising and fishing. The Film Society, with over 100 members, held its first staff film show during 1958 and undertook several of its own productions, now fondly remembered by many of those involved. The Choral Society had around twenty members and won warm praise for its singing at the annual staff dinner, usually held in the Royal Hibernian Hotel. The staff association football team maintained an almost unbeaten record right through the 1950s and included such stars as international Shamrock Rovers player Gerry Mackey and Jack Lyons, the amateur international.

This was also the era of the man who, of all the many sportsmen and women who have been part of the Shell organisation in Ireland, none would dispute was the greatest of them all. I refer, of course, to the great Christy Ring, whose eight All-Ireland medals were testament to the fact that this was the finest hurler ever to take the field. Christy had worked in the Cork Terminal before becoming a representative for the company. Never one to push himself forward, his personality seemed at odds with the outgoing sort of individual one normally associates with this role. That he was famously successful was due to the great respect he engendered and the deep love of sport in the Irish psychic.

Other staff activities included tennis, golf, rugby, horticulture and a gramophone society. Other locations around the country also had their own staff Social and Sports Clubs but worthy of particular note was the Dublin Installation Association, which was responsible for a wonderful Children's Christmas Party each year.

The inaugural dinner of a new society with the unusual title of 'The Badgers' took place in Dublin in 1958. The Badgers were established by members of staff with at least twenty-five years service. Each member of The Badgers was presented with a gold emblem. For every further five years an additional diamond was added. To Vincent M McCurdy, retired Installation Manager at Foynes, belonged the distinction of being the only person to possess an emblem studded with five diamonds. At the inaugural dinner of the group, chaired by Herbie James who had conceived the name 'Badgers', forty-seven employees with a combined service of 1,446 years were present.

Amongst the new intake of staff in the late 1950s was Terry Balfe, who joined the company as Sales Promotion and Advertising Representative and

Members of the Newly-formed
Dublin Golfing Association – 1957

Down through the years, Golf has been a constant pastime of the employees of Irish Shell. Photographed at Baltray Golf Course in 1957 were members of the then newly-formed Dublin Branch Golfing Association. From left standing: P C Creagh, T O'Loughlin. Seated: J J Lenehan, F G McArdle, J V Tighe (President), J D Buggle and D J McDonough.

was promoted to Supervisor of that Department in 1960. Prior to joining the company, Terry had been in the Irish Army where he reached the rank of Captain. Following his stint in the army, he had been involved in promotion work, most notably as the organising secretary of the Dublin An Tóstal celebrations Council, and had worked with advertising agency McConnells. A lovely, affable man, who got on well with everybody, Terry was also responsible for managing Irish Shell's involvement in Irish motor sport, of which the company was at the time one of the largest sponsors. Terry became, without doubt, one of the best-liked and most respected persons in Irish motor sport, where his gift of being able to mix business and pleasure successfully made his name synonymous with Shell.

Shell Voices

Cork Installation
I first joined the company in Dublin as an engineer. My starting salary in 1951 was £620 0s 0d per annum. My first assignment meant spending over three months in Cork. A new 'waterfed' installation was under construction on the Centre Park Road. A large tract of land had been acquired on which a sizeable tank farm was to be installed, as well as new offices, loading bays, stores and pump houses.

Instead of petroleum products being delivered to Cork by rail or road, seagoing tankers would now sail up the Lee from refineries in the UK and berth at Ford's wharf. Products would be pumped through pipelines and along the boundary of the Ford Motor Works, underneath Centre Park Road and into our new installation. Two Shell engineers from the UK had supervised the beginning of the project and I was sent down to take over from them and complete the job. This meant working very extended hours. I was not long in Cork before I made the acquaintance of some very interesting people, including Gerald Barry, a Shell/BP Sales Representative and a prominent member of the Sunday's Well Rugby Club and the Royal Munster (now Royal Cork) Yacht Club at Crosshaven. He introduced me to both organisations. Although diminutive in stature, he had been a famous full back in his time and had been selected for Munster. When I finished work at night I frequently called in to the Rob Roy pub for a few drinks – this establishment being the unofficial headquarters of Sunday's Well, where I was sure to meet up with Gerald and some of his colleagues. Gerald, who became a close friend and remained so until his death, was the best after dinner speaker I have ever heard and was in constant demand, even by the eloquent legal profession, to entertain guests at their functions.

Gerry O'Neill – Operations Manager

The Irish Board
There were always representatives of Shell-Mex and BP on the Board. The first I knew was Sir Fenton Hort, who was joined by Mr George Wilson, who I think was more interested in fishing than the oil business in Ireland, but I may be maligning him. The Irish Board always

New Authorised Distributor Depots – 1954

The appointment of Authorised Distributors from 1953 onwards saw the establishment of many new depots throughout the country. Typical of these depots were the South of Ireland Petroleum depots at Tallow in Waterford and Mallow in Cork. The large photograph shows the local storekeeper greeting the Irish Shell driver making the first bridging delivery to the Mallow Depot. The smaller right-hand photograph shows the same scene with E C Bourke, Irish Shell Branch Manager, Cork and Bill O'Brien of South of Ireland Petroleum Company in view. The left-hand photograph shows the Tullow Depot.

had the closest relations with London although the representation varied much as did the personalities of the people.

Lord Killanin (Recorded in 1984) – Director

The best Number

I started in 1955 as an Area Representative and before that I spent 4 years with Ferguson tractors and I got to know Shell very well and I said to myself, as far as I can see, Shell is about the best number that I can get into. It had a name as one of the best jobs in the country so I applied for a job as a representative in Dublin and was called for an interview and was given the job.

Jim Birmingham – Commercial Representative

A Good Day at Dublin Terminal

The office supervisor at Dublin Terminal, Michael Joyce was his name, Mr Joyce, you could never call him Michael Joyce, he was always Mr Joyce, he sat up on a high stool and one of his jobs was to draw the line on the book – you had to sign-in in the morning and he drew the line at five past nine... and you could be falling-in the door having turned the corner from Fairview into the East Wall on your bicycle and it would depend on which way the wind was blowing if you were going to be on time or not. Once five past nine came the line was drawn and you were below the line. It was a good day when you got in on time and didn't have a row with the switchboard operator!

Des Murphy – Personnel Manager

Oops!

The Fuel Oil and Bitumen site at Alexandra Road was built to enable Shell to bring in liquid bitumen, a product which had previously been brought in by barrel. The opening reception was in full swing and in conjunction with the opening of the site, Shell were also launching their own railcars. This was to facilitate Irish Shell delivering bitumen in bulk to County Councils around the country. Until this, they had used Port & Docks equipment so this was another great first. All were assembled for this – among them the manager of the site, a Mr O'Donoghue, and many others. With incredible timing the shunting engine veered to one side and went off the rails!

Leo O'Carroll – Manager, Dublin Terminal

The trouble with Bitumen rail-cars

There were always rows going on between the County Councils and the company over the rail-cars that were used to deliver the bitumen. The rail-cars were old and a pipe came down out of the tank and turned sideways. The idea was that the bitumen would gravity-feed into a tank or a lorry but the product in the pipe would go solid with the result that it would have to be poked free and usually one got splashed. Not very pleasant.

John Buggle – Special Trade Manager

Herb Elliott Visits

Herb Elliott paid a visit to Irish Shell House in August 1958. While in Ireland, Elliott, who was attached to Shell Chemical, Australia, shattered the world record for the mile at Santry Stadium when he returned a time of 3 minutes 54.5 seconds, bettering the existing record by almost three seconds. Elliott signed autographs for (from left): Louie Elliott, Catherine Kavanagh, Audrey Kereison, Clare Dumbleton, C McGatey and Cosie Harney.

Smoking in the Office

Of course you weren't allowed smoke in the office. If you wanted to smoke you had to go outside and there was a break at 10.30 in the morning for ten minutes and if anybody wanted to smoke then you went out on the road.

Des Murphy – Personnel Manager

At that time a number of the staff smoked in the office whilst working. One in particular was a bachelor named Tommy Loughman who was a thorough gentleman. His one fault was that he was a little untidy and the drawers of his desk were not always models of neatness. We had to price out deliveries by Authorised Distributors to customers where the account was held by ISBP. This could mean having in your desk drawers, bundles of dockets supported by the credit document to the AD. On one unfortunate occasion, Tommy, without knowing it, let a cigarette butt fall into a drawer and thought it had gone into the waste paper basket beside where he sat. Unfortunately, after about five or six minutes there was a smell of burning and when they opened the drawer a number of documents had gone on fire.

Needless to say, the poor man was terribly embarrassed and it took a while to live the comments down.

Paddy Dunne – Head Office Administration

Nixer Alley'

Between the yard at Dublin Terminal and the Motor Repair Centre there was an alley which ran along and this was 'Nixer Alley' because you had the carpenter here and the painter here and if you wanted anything done then that was the place to get it done.

Des Murphy – Personnel Manager

Branch Offices

During the 1950s significant changes took place. I was involved in most of these, which included the introduction of Authorised Distributors, and the formation of an outside organisation, Pump Services, which enabled all the major oil companies to dispense with the services of their pump fitters who were made redundant. During the 1950s era, a completely inept and costly exercise was forced upon us by our lords and masters across the channel. This was the setting up of three branch offices. Somebody at the top felt that Sales activities should be completely divorced from the Head Office and Distribution centre. A Cork Branch Office was set up in the South Mall, just below The Imperial Hotel, the Manager there being Ned Bourke, a somewhat austere man, who after reluctantly retiring at 60, joined the priesthood following the death of his wife. Another Branch Office was set up in Sligo, two of the Branch Managers being Arthur Henderson and then later, Niall O'Connell. The Dublin Branch Office was located in Lower O'Connell Street. The first Branch Manager being Bill Tate. On the death of Bill, Johnny Tighe, who had been Fuel and Lubricants Manager for about 22 years replaced Bill, and I was promoted from Fuel and Lubricants Supervisor in the Dublin Branch office to take over from Johnny Tighe in Fleet Street. Fortunately, the Branch Offices exercise didn't survive for very long.

Gerry O'Neill – Operations Manager

New Cork Installation – 1957

Pictured at the Official Opening of the Cork Terminal in 1957 were: From left, front row: Eugene Aherne, Irish Shell Branch Sales Supervisor; Commander George Crosbie, *Cork Examiner*; Lord Mayor Jago; Tom Crawford Young, Managing Director, Irish Shell; Jack Murphy, Sales Manager, Irish Shell; John Horgan, Contractor; – Crosbie, Cork Examiner. Others identified are Frank Blennerhassett, Kerry Petroleum; Noel Nunan, Operations Officer, Cork and Bill Moore, AD/K&A Superintendent.

"Tell Paddy I'll see him Tomorrow"

In Limerick there was a two faced pump in operation in a particular petrol station. I can recall an occasion when a customer asked for three gallons of petrol, which the attendant gave him, but the clock hands never registered at the customer side. As it so happened, I was making a delivery about two days later, and it was usual for the drivers to help out when there was a queue of cars waiting. I obliged this customer with four gallons of petrol, to which he said, "Tell Paddy I'll see him tomorrow". Of course, I took his number and told Paddy as requested. "Oh, you effin fool – that's that mad fellow again, who was discharged from the mental hospital last week!"

John 'Sean' McMahon, Lorry Boy and Driver

The Annual Children's Party

The Dublin Terminal Sports and Social Club used to run an annual children's party at Barry's Hotel. Eugene Lambert used to come along on his bicycle with a big brown suitcase on the carrier at the back inside which was his ventriloquist's dummy. He was paid ten shillings (50p) for doing his turn which he did for years.

Des Murphy – Personnel Manager

The Scrap-barrel Supervisor

In the 1950s and 1960s the staff (at Dublin Terminal) were all male with some characters amongst them – mostly good men – and my favourite was the late operative Thomas Barber – known to all as 'Tommo' – he was based at the F.O.B. site. He was a short, stocky man with a voice like a fog-horn. He was hopeless at the loading bays in the yard but was excellent at heavy jetty work, unloading tankers and bunkering vessels at the jetty side. He was always in good humour, slagging his work mates – nobody was spared – even captains he addressed as 'Whiskers'. In his later years, hundreds of empty lube oil barrels were returned to the terminal and he was very good at stacking them neatly in confined spaces – hence he was known as 'the Scrap-barrel Supervisor'. He also kept the canteen clean and tidy and after meal breaks he would – with well-chosen vocabulary – clear the canteen and tell the operatives to "get up the yard where I can see you walking around like statues".

Cormac McGuinness – Dublin Terminal Shipping Supervisor

Barney Byrne's Job

Barney Byrne was the boss out in the yard and you could do nothing without him. Friday was pay day and the money would come down by cheque from Head Office. Somebody would go up to the bank, take out all the money and three people would go up the Chief Clerk's office and all the envelopes were made up for the men. And the men would all be milling around out here and Barney Byrne's job was to keep them out there till the money was ready. When it was ready somebody would give him the word and he would open the door and call out "Come in here, you shower of animals!"

Des Murphy – Personnel Manager

Champions All!

The date was sometime in the 1950s and the venue was outside the Bank of Ireland in College Green, Dublin. All were Shell employees and all were outstanding sportsmen who gained distinction in their chosen field of excellence. Their contemporaries will recall them and their achievements. From left, they are: Paddy Berkery who played at Full Back for Lansdowne and Ireland; Gerry Mackey who was Centre Half for Shamrock Rovers and Ireland; Jackie Lyons played League of Ireland with Transport and Irish League Football with Glenavon; Paddy Prendergast was Full Back for Mayo and won 2 All-Irelands; Christy Ring who played for Cork winning 8 All-Irelands and Ken Hill who played Table Tennis for Ireland.

First in the Field

I was working in Portland, Oregon, for a timber company there with a view to coming back to Ireland and getting a job with a timber broker. While in New Orleans, I met a number of young American graduates who were training with Shell and they gave me an insight into what life was like with Shell. I decided that this was where my future lay. So when I came back to Ireland in 1959, I made application to all the oil companies. I was successful with Irish Shell and they took me on as a trainee superintendent at the sum of £750 per annum. I spent three months training with Shell Mex and BP in the UK and then I came back to Ireland and joined the Fuel Oil Department where I was one of the team responsible for developing the domestic heating market in Ireland, which was then in its infancy. Shell, incidentally, was the first company to see the potential of that market and was first in the field in Ireland.

Basil Carr – Retail Promotions and Advertising Manager

Young versus Youth

I recall Jackie Lyons telling me that a few days after he started he was in the Order/Routing office around lunch hour when the phone rang. He picked it up to hear "Young here" to which he replied "Young who" not knowing it was Crawford Young the MD on the line. When Young enquired as to who that was answering the phone, Jackie realised his indiscretion and promptly hung up. Naturally, an inquiry followed but Crawford Young never found out who the young fellow was.

Gerry Gilmore – Authorised Distributor Manager

Under Pressure

Around the mid 1950s, there was the mad rush by all the companies to sign loyalty contracts and soon followed the race to purchase and develop company owned sites. For the first time in its history, the Company, I suspect, experienced serious competition, and hence, a measure of field staff accountability was introduced and indeed, some staff 'transfers' quickly emerged. I was involved administratively in the new service station finance set-up, before being appointed Internal Auditor in 1960 – a function now far removed from the days of "counting the horseshoe nails". *The use of a company car was a big plus; less so the climbing of main terminal storage tanks. How not to make enemies is, I suppose, the first principle for internal auditors – unavoidable at times.*

Paddy Foley – Retail Services Manager

Terry Balfe

In those days, there were some great characters in ShelL people like Terry Balfe, who was in the Irish Army during 'The Emergency' and who joined Irish Shell from McConnell Hartley, which was the subsidiary of McConnells, the advertising agency. He was a man who was originally responsible for getting 'An Tóstal' off the ground. Terry became advertising manager at Irish Shell and was also responsible for sponsorship and motor sport.

Basil Carr – Retail Promotions and Advertising Manager

Aer Lingus 1,000,000th Passenger

Friday 13th of August, 1951 turned out to be a lucky day for Joan Curran, who was then a shorthand typist with Irish Shell, when she became the 1,000,000 passenger to be flown by Aer Lingus. Upon embarking on a Douglas Dakota flight to Heathrow, London, Joan was presented with a special medallion and a box of chocolates by Captain Kelly-Rogers who was then the Chief Pilot of Aer Lingus and who had been involved in several of the great pioneering flights from Foynes some years earlier.

121

'The Node'

The company laid great store on training and development of personnel. I attended several courses in the UK, mainly at Shell Mex House on the Strand in London and also at 'The Node', a very imposing mansion set in beautiful surroundings in rural Hertfordshire, close to the village of Coddicote.

Gerry O'Neill – Operations Manager

The Shell and BP Fleet

In 1957 I was fortunate enough to be called for an interview with Irish Shell, Fleet Street, and two weeks later took up employment at Alexandra Road. The interviewers were Mr Edward Gavin, Transport Engineer and Mr L S Murdoch, Staff Supervisor. The first thing of note on going to Alexandra Road was that trains ran down the centre of the road, something like one would see in Western films. Also, I thought that many of the men there were very old. I now realise that they were in their mid-fifties and now I would consider that 'young'. However, that's how it appeared to a twenty-six year old.

The Shell and BP fleet consisted mainly of Bedford artics with 2,000 gallon semi-trailers. A few 4,000 gallon Mammoth Majors, AEC Monarchs, Leyland Octopuses with vacuum assisted hydraulic brakes, American Internationals with petrol engines and some Gardiner engined Scammels drawing bitumen to Newry. All of them lacked the luxury of power steering and manoeuvring in a tight space was hard work. Cab heaters had not yet caught on and trucks were very noisy inside and out compared with today. The colour scheme was a green cab and a red cargo tank. The Company had two installations, the second of which was then known as "the new site". F.O.B. was right at the end of Alexandra Road and if you went any further you were in the tide. How it has since changed with huge areas of ground reclaimed from the sea.

Vincent Sheridan – Inspector Motor Mechanic

Frank Smith

When I joined, I joined engineers and for a period we had facilities at Dublin Terminal, or as we called it in those days, Dublin Installation. My immediate boss was the engineer, Frank Smith, who was based at Dame Street (Head Office) and who was a really nice fellow in every way, a very understanding man, fantastic as a boss, and of course, you could talk to him.

Alfie Duff – Engineering Assistant

We didn't need another small business...

The tractors were the start of our business. That led to the Oil business. Really, you know, it took me a good time to make up my mind because we didn't need another small business that was going to be a nuisance and it looked like that in the beginning, something they wanted to get rid of up there. You see they weren't prosperous times either, going back to that period of the 1950s. They were tough times so you had to give it a lot of thought. I didn't want to put too much money into it. I didn't either. They gave us a month's credit and that

Road and Rail Transport

Some of the road and rail transport used during the period from the early 1950s to the late 1980s was as follows: Top row from left – A Thames Trader Direct Delivery Tanker used for household deliveries prior to the establishment of the Authorised Distributor Network in 1954; A Bulk Lube Oil Delivery Lorry – also from the 1950s. Second row – One of the Aviation Service Tankers used for a period in the early 1950s to draw aviation fuel ex Foynes to Dublin Airport which had then insufficient storage facilities; A Leyland Beaver Tanker and Trailer unit. Third row – Three Leyland tankers together with an AEC Mammoth Major photographed at Dublin Airport. Bottom row – A Leyland 5000 litre Fuel Oil Tanker and finally, (on left) Herbie James and Sean O'Brien take delivery of a new Irish Shell and BP Rail Tanker at CIE's Inchicore Works in 1971

was it, but you see credit goes out very fast. We took over their trucks and then we bought a few more as time went on and kept it moving that way but it worked out okay. Its turned into a huge business. I don't know how many times it's quadrupled. You know, they deliver more in a day than we did in a year.

Frank Blennerhassett – Retired Authorised Distributor (Kerry Petroleum).

Oh, what a lovely War!
As I got to know the men, I found them to be great characters and very funny. Some had served at El Alamein and other hot spots. Driver Bill Moore was a prisoner-of-war courtesy of Adolf Hitler and his experiences were fascinating. Jimmy Pike, chauffeur to the Managing Director "had a great war, went right up through Italy and never encountered a Jerry" *but apparently encountered some luscious Italian women.*

Vincent Sheridan – Inspector Motor Mechanic

Out of the frying pan into the fire...
Well, I must confess that when I joined the Company, I assumed that I was going to be working in Dublin because the previous company that I was working with, I was only with them a couple of years but the reason that I was keen to leave was that I discovered that a lot of work in the country was involved, which I didn't want because at that time I was in the CBSI in Dún Laoghaire, I played football, I did a bit of cycling and in general I'd no time to go to the country, as I thought. So, I don't really know how it came about, I know I had a friend in Shell and maybe that influenced me a bit, so I applied and had an interview with Frank Smith and joined the Company in August 1949 assuming that I would grow an old man in Dublin! In September, I was given my first move. I was being sent to Enniscorthy and to Waterford. Honest to God, this is a right start, I thought, I've just walked out of the frying pan into the fire. Anyway, they sent me away and at the last moment they decided that they had better send an experienced person with this fellow to show him around so they set me up with one of the older fellows, a chap by the name of Bill Craddock, long since dead, who was very kind...he showed me the ropes, he had the responsibility and as well as that he had transport, so I thought this country work's not so bad after all, I just do what Bill tells me to do. It was quite nice, you know, I even got home for the weekend, so I was very pleased with all this. October I got another call. I was to go to Bantry. Well, I was convinced that Bantry was somewhere on the 49th Parallel. So anyway, I was going to Bantry and it was so far away and I'd no transport and I had to travel by train but in those days everything was left to you. You had to make your own arrangements. I had to go home and get a map to see was Bantry in this country at all, I needed to know if I needed a passport!

So anyway, I made a few enquiries. Apparently, the Cork train left at ten to eleven in the morning so I was there about an hour early having left Dún Laoghaire at nine o'clock. I was looking after all the bits and pieces that I had to bring with me, which you were totally responsible for yourself. Eventually, the train pulled into Glanmire where everybody else got off. I thought maybe they're switching, so I got off the train and met a porter and I said "By the way, do we go from a different platform". "Where're you going," *he said. So I said*

Shannon Airport – Shell Aviation Service

A Hydrant Refuelling Service was introduced at Shannon Airport in 1956. The introduction of a system of pipes and hydrant points at each of the aircraft 'stands' allowed fuel to be always 'on tap' and did away with the need for tanker vehicles having to return to their base to refuel. In the main photograph, a Lockeed Constellation of Lufthansa is being refuelled using the Hydrant system.
The other photographs show some of the Shannon Airport personnel (clockwise from top left): Alfie Duff; Jimmy Donoghue; Jimmy Donoghue, Morgan Bourke, Leo Dygnam, Alfie Duff and Pat Halpin; Alfie Duff; Aidan Guilfoyle, Jack Hassatt and Alfie Duff.

125

"Bantry". "Ah sure, the train doesn't go to Bantry from here – it goes from Albert Quay". "Where's Albert Quay", *I says*. "Well, if you go out of here now and take the first turn on the left and continue on for about a hundred yards then bear right and go over the bridge, turn left again and continue on". "Hold on", *I said*, "I'm not walking to Bantry!"

Alfie Duff – Engineering Assistant

Giving the overcoat as well as the suit

When we took over, I thought there was a good deal of gas oil but unfortunately most of it went into some drainage scheme in North Kerry and we lost all that when the scheme was finished. So we ended up with no gas oil or very little but it was beginning to come back when the diesel tractor came out. We had a ready market because if we sold a tractor we had a customer so that counted. We could give the overcoat as well as the suit. That way we built up a good connection.

Frank Blennerhassett – Retired Authorised Distributor (Kerry Petroleum).

Head Office in the mid-1950s

I joined in 1955 and before that I worked in an Accountant's office and I had done Chartered Secretary's exams so I was a Chartered Secretary before I went into the Company. At that time Tom Crawford Young had a secretary, Vivienne Till, (who had also been secretary to Hugh Harpur) and who had been there a long, long time and she was retiring – at that time ladies retired at 55 and the men at 60 – and her time had come and so she was retiring. Instead of moving somebody up they decided to bring in somebody from outside so I had a few interviews with Tom Crawford Young and Walter Joyce, who was the Assistant General Manager Administration, and then eventually I was accepted and I started in September 1955. Actually, I was interviewed in July but a strike occurred in the Terminal around that time so there was a big gap before I started work in Head Office at Fleet Street.

Everybody was very nice to me and I loved the job but I found it very difficult because everybody knew me and I knew nobody, and it was hard to get to know people as they were on four different floors. At that time, Fred Dixon was the Assistant General Manager Marketing and he was a great character, a big man who loved racing; Dick Sinnott was the Secretary and the Operations Manager was a man from Scotland called George Coutts while Bill Murdoch was the Personnel Manager. Nancy Mulligan was his Secretary.

Carmel Mallaghan – Secretary to Tom Crawford Young

"Kicking over the Bucket"

I joined Irish Shell & BP Limited as it was then in 1958, based in 13/16 Fleet Street, when the organisation was under the stewardship of T A Crawford Young, ably supported by Fred Dixon.

Initially, I was assigned to the Pricing & Stocks Department. During my time there, I was processing tickets covering Bunkerings. As most Bunkering accounts would be either held by SMBP, as it was then, or one of the parent companies, there was no duty chargeable.

Assemblers Service Station at Townsend Street, Dublin

State-of-the-art petrol retailing in 1958, the newly developed Shell Service Station at Townsend Street, Dublin.

Opened by Ferrari World Champion, Mike Hawthorn, only a few weeks before his tragic death in a road accident, the Assemblers Service Station at Townsend Street, Dublin, represented State-of-the-art petrol retailing in 1958. The lower picture shows Mike Hawthorn (on left) and Ernest Bell of Assemblers Ltd. at the opening of the new Service Station.

*However, on one occasion, there were some sales to a ship where the account was held in Ireland and in this case duty, which I think at that time was one old penny per gallon, was chargeable. Well, yours truly didn't price the ticket accordingly and omitted the duty and the invoice was raised. It later, of course, came to light when the customer queried it and there was quite a furore. Mr Tom O'Carroll was the Office Manager at the time and Norman Pappin was the Section Head. The whole section was called up to the Office Manager's room, including myself, and after a long dressing down, he ended the interview by stating that "*we were like the good cow which when she had given good milk kicked over the bucket."* Needless to say, there was great difficulty in keeping our faces straight and for quite a long time afterwards, it was a source of banter in the section.*

Paddy Dunne – Head Office Administration

Sir Mr Young!
Mr T A Crawford Young was Managing Director and he was regarded not only with great respect but with a reverence perhaps tinged with a little fear. I remember my first Christmas Eve there seeing the old hands trying to look busy and at the same time keeping their hands clean in anticipation of his customary visit to shake hands and wish – Badgers only – a Happy Christmas, also their state of elation afterwards. A year or two later the stage was set and the whisper came "He's coming through the store"*. However times were changing and Mr Young didn't come into the workshop but paused in passing to greet Freddy Fox who was at the bench, with* "Happy Christmas Fox" *in a slightly raised and authoritative voice. Poor Freddy ran towards the door, tripping over the anvil on the way, whipped off his cap and swept the floor with it and bowed double to exclaim,* "Many happy returns, Sir Mr Young"*. Freddy was lame for a week from the injury he received to his shin.*

I remember Mick Maguire and Joe Coffey telling about when drivers retired they had to hand in the company issue overcoat. This rule was eventually amended and from then on the Shell buttons were cut off and retained by the company, whilst the poor man on his last day walked up Alexandra Road endeavouring to keep his buttonless coat wrapped around him.

Vincent Sheridan – Inspector Motor Mechanic

That was his Style
Crawford Young came down to Cork and I drilled the fellas that the Boss was coming and that he'd march around because although he was Managing Director he had been Equipment Manager and he'd checked everything. So, it was a boiler house I knew he was after and I told Tommy Cremin to have it shining for this man coming in because I knew his style. Anyway, he arrived and he marched into the Boiler House and the brasswork was gleaming and he just saw a dirty rag and he turned around to me and the other fella and he said "I expect to be able to have my dinner off the floor of this place every time I come down"*. That was his style.*

William Moore – Government Relations

Shell and B.P. Farm Services on Show – 1958

Shell and BP Farm Services were, from an early stage of the company's history, responsible for an important market and participated in several of the larger Agricultural Shows throughout the country. The Shell and BP Farm Services stand at the 1958 Cork Agricultural Show is pictured manned by Dan Daly and William Moore.

What will I say?

I also worked with a man called Michael Bannon who was a gentleman bachelor who lived with his sisters in Clontarf. He was friendly with Ken Hill and Tony Alvey and at that time went home for lunch every day with them – again indicative of the times we lived in. He never liked to be called anything else but Michael and didn't like bad language or innuendo and with characters like Wally Scott and Jimmy Cosgrave there were many instances where they would try to annoy Michael particularly by calling him Mickey B. On one particular occasion, the phone rang and either Jimmy or Wally called out, "Mickey, there's a woman in reception with a child in her arms asking for you. What will I say?" *Needless to say, there was uproar and for a long time Michael refused to talk to any of the lads in the section.*

Paddy Dunne – Head Office Administration

Irish Shell Wildfowl Calendar – 1968

Throughout the 1950s and 1960s, Irish Shell produced an enormous amount of nature related material for use in schools. Hardly a school in Ireland didn't have a selection of Shell Wall-charts and the annual Shell Wildlife calendar hanging from its walls. Today, this material is fondly remembered by several generations of children who attended school during that time.

En route to Valentia Island – 1959

Irish Shell has always been conscious of the needs of our island communities, and this photograph, taken in 1959, shows Jack McCarthy, the Irish Shell Agent at Cahirciveen, County Kerry, with the ferryman while crossing to Valentia Island, a journey all in a day's work for this Shell representative.

Blessing the Fleet – 1954

A common practice in the early 1950s when this picture was taken, Archbishop Joe Walsh blesses the fleet of Western Petroleum at Headford. Also in the photograph are Noel Maguire and Lord Killanin.

Recording Irish Shell 1958

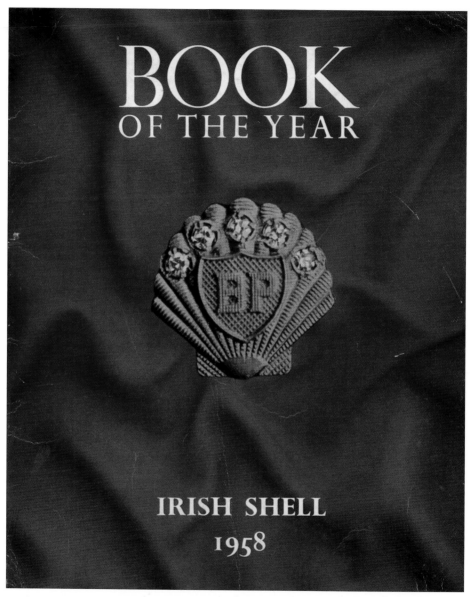

In 1958 Irish Shell published a 48 page 'Book of the Year' giving an overview of Shell operations in Ireland as well as looking at some of the country's key industries. Lavishly produced for the time, the book today provides a valuable insight into the workings of the company. Its cover portrayed the emblem worn by members of the Badgers – an association formed in 1958 by long-service employees of Irish Shell. After twenty-five years' service, an employee was presented with this emblem by the company, and for every five years service thereafter, a diamond was inserted in the badge.

The Weston Air Displays

In the 1950s, private aviation in Ireland underwent a revival at Weston Aerodrome, near Leixlip, where the Aero Club of Ireland was based. The series of air displays begun in 1955 by the Club attracted huge crowds and helped generate a new interest in aviation amongst the Irish public. Irish Shell provided refuelling facilities at Weston and two of the company's vehicles are seen in the top photograph refuelling a DH Dragon. In the lower photograph are the Irish Shell personnel (from left): Des Ryan, Brendan Foster and John Lally.

Chapter 6

The 1960s:
Under Pressure

On September 1st 1961, Irish Shell changed its name to Irish Shell and BP, the change being reflected in this new combined logo.

1960-1969 Boland President of the United Nations – Irish UN troops killed in the Congo – RTE begins transmissions – Theatre Royal demolished – President Kennedy visits Ireland – President Kennedy assassinated – Nelson's Pillar blown up – Lemass meets O'Neill at Stormont – Foot and Mouth restrictions – The Beatles become popular – Yom Kippur War – Traffic Wardens appear for the first time on Dublin Streets – Civil Rights Movement in USA

The first Government Inquiry into the Retail Motor business was held during 1959 and 1960. Its background could be traced back to the early days of petrol retailing when most petrol retailers were mixed retailers, selling several different petrol brands from the same forecourt. Eventually, the oil industry had introduced the Solus Agreement, with the intention of ensuring that they had outlets for their products. The Inquiry was mainly concerned with assessing whether the Solus system was in the public interest. In its report published in 1961, the Fair trade Commission held that on balance the Solus system had considerable merit in facilitating the rationalisation of distribution. The Inquiry prohibited wholesalers from price differentiating between one Solus retailer and another and in addition restricted Solus agreements to a term of five years.

On September 1st 1961, Irish Shell Limited made yet another change to its name, becoming Irish Shell and BP Limited. The change was brought about by the coming together of the Shell and BP organisations in Ireland. Both brands continued, however, to retain distinct personalities. For example, there continued to be BP as well as Shell petrol filling stations, an arrangement which continued until the two companies were finally de-merged in 1976.

On the sporting front, 1961 saw Shell in the USA launch the Shell Wonderful World of Golf, a series designed to bring top quality golf on world-class courses to the general public. The series coincided with the rapid expansion of television ownership in Ireland and was an immediate success. Matches were played throughout the world and were filmed for television transmission including three in Ireland featuring Harry Bradshaw, Joe Carr and Christy O'Connor. And although the initial series only continued until 1970, it had a lasting impact on the burgeoning number of golfers in Ireland who had come to associate Shell with the Wonderful World of Golf, an association which continues strongly to this day.

As the 1960s progressed Shell enjoyed an unprecedented period of growth in its business. The economic miracle begun in the 1950s under Sean Lemass was gathering strength and a new confidence was abroad in Irish business. Several shrewd investments in plant and facilities by Irish Shell were now bearing fruit. In particular, the company's bitumen business was booming, while its commercial business counted among its customers all of the country's major enterprises. Irish Shell were suppliers to all of the Electricity Supply Board's power stations and imported special transformer oils from France for the flag-ship power project at Turlough Hill in County Wicklow, then just coming on-line. Another huge customer at this time was Clondalkin Paper Mills as well as most of the country's Co-ops and Fisheries and it can truly be said that customers were queuing up to secure supplies of Shell products during this time of unprecedented expansion. Apart from its terminals, Irish Shell had around 35 depots strategically sited throughout the country as well as the bitumen plant at Dublin. Undoubtedly, these facilities helped the company to gain a significant advantage over its rivals in the development of its commercial business, something it retains to this day.

When Tom Crawford Young retired on March 31st 1964, he was a year over the mandatory retirement age, but had been asked to stay on for an additional year. An austere man, he had been greatly respected – if perhaps slightly feared – but then, that was the norm of the times. Tom Crawford Young died in June 1993 just a month short of his 90th birthday.

Bernard Nolan

Bernard Nolan succeeded Tom Crawford Young as Managing Director of Irish Shell and BP in 1964. A man of deep intellect, he took the company through the difficult years of de-merger from BP and the industrial turmoil of the 1970s. He was, in turn, succeeded by Jim Beveridge in 1981.

His departure from the role of Managing Director drew to a close another era of Irish Shell's history. What followed became more and more the history of the modern company and the actions taken in succeeding years have served to largely shape the company that exists today.

The man chosen to succeed Tom Crawford Young as Managing Director was Bernard A Nolan, who, having graduated from UCD in Civil Engineering, spent some twelve years in general engineering before joining Irish Shell in 1955. There followed a period as Operations Manager of the company in the 1950s before working for Shell-Mex in the UK in the early part of the 1960s. A man of deep intellect, he had a strong commitment to the development of Irish Industry and business.

Towards the end of 1966, Irish Shell and BP acquired the long established business of Munster Simms, who had been an independent supplier of a range of oil products since the early part of the century. In a move which was regarded as pre-empting the arrival of a major not then active in the Irish market, the business and employees of Munster Simms were absorbed into Irish Shell. In June 1967, the Yom Kippur or Six-Day War in the Middle East closed the Suez Canal for the first time since the Suez Crisis in 1956. Oil supplies for Europe had as a result to travel by the Cape of Good Hope causing a dramatic rise in oil prices, although adroit planning by Irish Shell staff averted a major supply crisis here.

In 1968, staff of Irish Shell and BP throughout the country were shocked to learn that a colleague, Noel Nunan, had been amongst those lost when an Aer Lingus Viscount crashed near Tuskar Rock while flying from Cork to London. Noel, who had been Branch Operations Supervisor based at the Cork terminal, was survived by his wife, Mary, and a young family.

At the end of the 1960s, two long-standing practices amongst the oil companies came to an end. Gerry O'Neill takes up the story:

In the late 1960s, Operations Managers in the major oil companies got together to try to hammer out a deal with the unions, with the object of eliminating these 'Spanish Customs' – the principal objectives being the elimination of bogus overtime and the more economical deployment of our transport fleets. With my colleagues from Esso, Texaco, McMullans and Burmah, we embarked on discussions with the Unions, which went on incessantly for two years. In the end, we achieved a satisfactory deal. We were able to introduce a two shift system. A lot of drivers would start at 6.00 am and work until 2.00 pm, when another shift would take over the vehicles and work until 10.00 pm, thus giving about 16 hours of effective work out of each

Noel Nunan

Noel Nunan was an employee of Irish Shell at its Cork terminal when he was tragically lost in the crash of an Aer Lingus Viscount near Tuskar Rock. The Viscount was flying from Cork to London where Noel was due to attend a Shell training course. Noel is remembered as a quiet and pleasant individual whose tragic death was a great shock to all his colleagues.

vehicle. The drivers also agreed to drive at more sensible and realistic speeds. We introduced Saturday working, on the same basis as weekdays. Overtime was eliminated under the new scheme. There were, however, a few cases where deliveries had to be made to points a long distance away from base, which could involve a few hours overtime. To overcome this, we offered a ten hour day, four day week, with three days off each week. After some hesitation, this was accepted.

The lorry boys were also dispensed with. All in all, the new system was a great benefit to the companies involved, although we had to pay a lot of extra money for its acceptance.

The sixties also saw the extension of company owned sites throughout the network. By contrast to today, a typical petrol station at that time consisted of a single petrol island supported by a workshop where motorists could have their car serviced. By extending the number of company owned sites, the major oil companies were now attempting to ensure outlets for their brands in the future. Very often, the company had suitable land for sites but lacked the capital to develop the property. Coincidentally, the motor trade at this time was experiencing rapid growth with car sales rising as the economy developed. The result was a marriage of convenience, if not quite a marriage made in Heaven! Jointly developed sites often ran into difficulties as the profit from car sales was considerably greater than that from petrol with the result that forecourts were given over to car display thus often blocking petrol pump access for Shell customers.

A spectacular fire in the early hours of the August Bank Holiday Monday at the Trim Road, Navan, Depot of Leinster Petroleum – one of Irish Shell's Authorised Distributors – made the headlines in 1969. The fire started at around 2.00 am and Fire Brigades from Navan, Trim, Kells and Drogheda were at the scene fighting the blaze for over eight hours. The fire, which was witnessed by large numbers of dancers from the nearby Beechmount Ballroom, was confined to one corner of the Depot by the firefighters but despite their efforts, three oil tankers, six storage tanks and a large quantity of oil were destroyed before the fire was brought under control.

The decade of the sixties ended with another initiative which was to endure into the future, Operation Clean-Sweep. This was a national competition designed to improve standards of presentation, efficiency and service at Irish Shell and BP sites throughout the country. A success right from the first year, Operation Clean-Sweep continued until recent times as the annual Shell Shine Competition.

Limerick Depot Opening – 1961

Work on a new Limerick Depot began in July 1960 and was completed 15 months later at a cost of £300,000. The development made possible the delivery of products from the refinery at Whitegate, Co. Cork, and from Shell and BP refineries in the UK, by coastal tankers including the Irish-registered Irish Holly *which was on long-term charter to Irish Shell and BP. The photographs show (clockwise from top left): a general view of the new Depot; the* Irish Holly *bringing the first cargo to the new Depot; the entrance to the Depot showing the office area and a tanker at the new loading gantry.*

Finally, before leaving the 1960s, mention must be made of the Shell Make Money petrol promotion in 1966. The promotion was simplicity itself, Shell customers received a sealed envelope with half of a Make Money note inside. The notes were of various values from £1 up to the top prize of £10,000 and the idea gripped the Irish public's imagination like no other promotion, before or since, has ever done. At the height of the Make Money promotion, the classified advertising columns of the evening papers were full of advertisements from people seeking their 'missing half'. The Make Money promotion achieved an extraordinary increase in market share for Irish Shell and was repeated with similar results in the 1980s. Its success gave rise to many other promotions down the years.

Shell Voices

Changes
With the 1960s came some measure of prosperity. People took out mortgages for new houses, some abandoned their bikes for cars. Television pushed the transistor radio which was 'the thing' before then into second place. Domestic washing machines replaced the washboard and tub. Central Heating gained in popularity and in anticipation of the trend, Irish Shell ads. gave a preview of Mrs 1970. Munster Simms was merged in the late 1960s. Brand separation came when Shell and BP were no longer allies but competitors. Productivity was introduced and brought many changes. Computers, (were) at first only in a special room in Hatch Street.

Vincent Sheridan – Inspector Motor Mechanic

Jack of all Trades
Tom Barber worked in the F.O.B. site and a more conscientious worker you could not meet. It is fair to say that Tom never used a pen or pencil to record anything at work. He would merely relay the information to someone else who would write it down for him. Tom was as strong as an ox. He was not very tall but his limbs and chest were large. I saw him lift and drag ships' hoses on his own. It took four others to move them. He did various jobs around the place and I have many fond memories of Tom at work, but one I recall involved a load of returned empty barrels. You see, at one time there were a number of different values on returned empty barrels and it was a bit of a problem sorting them out particularly as they came back in CIE wagons with 60 or 70 on board from many different customers. I suspect some others just counted and advised the office the total number all at the current value. Not so with Tom. This very hot summer's day I was passing by this 'H' Railway wagon – this was a covered wagon with doors on both sides – and I heard this clanging and banging with barrels flying out either door on both sides accompanied by a roar from Tom, "£3"; "Foreign"(these had no value at all); "Damaged"; "F—-all for that" and so on until the

Sligo Occasions

Sligo staff and their spouses, pictured (top) at a presentation party on the occasion of Arthur Henderson's departure as Branch Manager in 1965. The second photograph shows Sligo staff at a dinner held in the Great Southern Hotel, Sligo in July 1954, just prior to the appointment of Authorised Distributors in the area. Present in the picture are, from top left: Patsy Gallagher, Mr House (UK), D L Ryan, Tom Crawford Young, James Murphy, Walter Joyce, Bill Murdoch, M J Murphy, John Mooney, Ned Tiernan, Niall O'Connell, Tommy Curran, unidentified, Ernie Doyle, Sonny Duignan, unidentified, Des Ryan, Mr Ponsonby, Mick Guckian, Jim Kennedy, Bert Fleming, Paddy Kielty, Michael O'Brien, Martin Devins, John Leydon, Paddy Hanley, Steve Lynch, Charlie Gallagher, Charlie Coyle, M J Geary, unidentified and Jack Byron. Also present but not photographed were Dobby McManamy, Mick Patten, Roddy Lamb and Hyacinth Connolly.

wagon was empty. This he did unaware of me listening, not that he would care anyway. He was proud to be a Shell man and no one was going to put one over on him.

Gerry Gilmore – Authorised Distributor Manager

The Straightest Man I Ever Met

Tom Crawford Young was the straightest man I ever met, he was the kind of man who wouldn't tell a lie to save his life and he hated anybody to tell him a lie. I don't think he was religious but he had a tragedy in his life when his only son died of meningitis. He hated to owe money and would almost pay an account before the bill came. If something happened in the office and you tried to cover it up and he found out then he would have it in for you but if you told him what was wrong he would always help. He had no time for people who tried to pull the wool over his eyes, he was very sharp. He was very kind to anyone who was ill. A lot of people thought he was very brusque because he didn't mince his words. He worked really hard. He would come in and do his work and expected everybody else to do their work. He had his eye everywhere and knew what was going on. I found him very fair.

Carmel Mallaghan – Secretary to Tom Crawford Young

An All-rounder

Jack McCarthy was a real old-timer. He was a batchelor living with his sister. He ran a pub, he was a cattle-dealer and he was in the oil business and a great all-rounder. He would put on his clean shirt and collar and tie and he would come out with me and we'd go over to the Islands. There was great business down there, especially lube oil to the Spanish fishermen in Bantry and also just outside Cahirciveen.

William Moore – Government Relations

The Badgers

Employees on completing twenty-five years service were presented with a gold badge in the shape of the Shell emblem, and would proudly proclaim themselves as 'Badgers'. A diamond was added for each for each additional five years service. There were a few who liked to make it known that they were "Old BP men" and took great pride in their origins. The late Ben Hackett told me that he had worked in a forge in Sheriff Street where he shod Shell horses which delivered two gallon cans of 'spirit' from a four wheel cart. The word 'petrol' was rarely used in the terminal, always 'spirit'. When the horses were replaced by 'motor lorries', Ben was taken on at Alexandra Road.

Vincent Sheridan – Inspector Motor Mechanic

Adding BP to the name

Another change was the addition of "& BP" to the name of Irish Shell in 1961. Through the economic war period of the 1930s, the "BP" had, I think, been dropped as indeed had the globes on the pumps been altered as the Union Jack which went with the BP logo attracted some unwelcome attention. Although Shell-Mex and BP had been 'married' in the twenties

The First Pensioners Reunion – 1963

The first reunion of retired male members of staff of Irish Shell and BP in the Dublin area took place in 1963 at the North Star Hotel. The two oldest members present were Bob Shepard and John Brennan – both then sprightly seventy-nine year olds. From left (front row) those present were: J Tighe, J McPhilips, C Ramsey, H C Blee, R Toal, F Dixon, J Nolan. Second row: S Wilson, B Hackett, J Pratt, L Conway, J Maher, L O'Carroll, A Lawlor, N E McDonald, unknown, W Ashton, unknown. Back row: J O'Rourke, R Sheppard, J J Delahoyde, J Brennan, J Stewart, B Byrne, unknown, unknown, E Gavin, unknown, L Murdock, B Gilligan, P Lawrence, J McStay.

Shell Children's Christmas Parties – *c.* 1960

The Shell Children's Christmas Parties were a feature of the 1950s and '60s. Our photograph shows the Cahill sisters (children of Martin J Cahill), Geraldine, Bernadette, Louise, Carmel and Patricia, enjoying the 1960 party.

And at a Limerick Depot Childrens Party is 'Santa' McMahon with his two daughters, Peggy and Helen. To the right is Martin O'Doherty, a driver at Limerick.

and operated under that name in the United Kingdom and Africa, they were rivals. I really think the marriage was only consummated in quite recent times by the divorce.

Lord Killanin (Recorded in 1984) – Director

"I'm very fond of the Jigs and Reels"
We had a driver in the Wexford area who delivered kerosene to the farmers and co-ops and he was a bit of a wheeler-dealer. He had sidelines like a lot of people and anyway, he got in serious trouble and Jack Murphy was sent down to him. There were a lot of complaints about him from Head Office, there were no stock returns in and he wasn't collecting his accounts. Jack gave him a dressing-down and the fellow didn't like it at all "Its like this, Mr Murphy", he says, "When I'm coming back of an evening I can't pass the Dance Hall. I'm very fond of the jigs and the reels and that's what delays me, I just couldn't get back to do my stock returns and that's the only excuse I can give you". So Jack went away wondering what he was going to put into his written report to Head Offiice.

William Moore – Government Relations

'Cha-Cha' and 'Bag-pipes'
There were many 'characters' working at Dublin Terminal during the 1960s and many of these were operatives. It appeared that they all had nicknames and it took a newcomer some time to match the face to the name. One I recall was Joe Keeley, a checker in the Lub Oil warehouse. He was called 'Bag-pipes' by his workmates. Joe was from Scotland – hence the nickname – and a lovely man he was, Lord rest him. Joe was responsible for recording all movements of lubricants, churns and lubricant oil barrels into and out of the warehouse and he carried out his duties extremely conscientiously if somewhat seriously. Another checker was Charlie 'Cha-Cha' O'Grady, who did his job well but always with a twinkle in his eye. Returns would arrive into the yard and if Cha-Cha counted them he would advise Bag-pipes who would record the items on the warehouse sheet and would always say "thank you". However, when the coast was clear, Bag-pipes would disappear from sight – as he thought – and Cha-Cha would regularly observe him doing his own count on the same items, just to satisfy himself that the information was correct. You see, it was P J Keeley's own signature that was going on all the documents. This practice continued during all the years they worked harmoniously together and were the best of friends.

Gerry Gilmore – Authorised Distributor Manager

Car Parks
An important operational innovation introduced during my period with ISBP was undertaken; this was the 'Car Park' system of transporting our products to outlying areas of the country. We acquired land outside Kells and Kinnegad, which we enclosed and installed a small office. We also used facilities at Kilkenny and Carrick-on-Shannon, to participate in the new distribution system. Our transport fleet at this time was changing over from the fixed lorry type of vehicle to the tractor and trailer type. These latter types were despatched from Dublin Terminal to the four points mentioned above, where the full trailers were

Talented People

The 'Shell Multigraders' was the title of this group of talented musicians and singers pictured in action at the Irish Shell Social and Sports Club Dinner in 1961. They are (from left standing): Matt Feddis, Arthur Henderson, Bert Crosland, Pat Purcell, Kevin Hayes and seated: Alan Walsh, Aidan O'Carroll and J Cosgrave.

The second photograph shows the team from Irish Shell and BP's Head Office who took part in Question Time, the team quiz programme in the Joe Linnane Radio Show. Team members were (from left): Michael Higgins, Joe Duffy, Niall Purcell and Aidan O'Flanagan. Incidentally, their opponents were a team from the Irish Dunlop Company and the result was a draw.

detached and the tractor would return to Dublin with an empty trailer. Local drivers at the 'Car Parks' would undertake onward distribution of product to customers in outlying areas. This system of distribution meant the elimination of many of our small country depots, most of which became part of the AD network.

Gerry O'Neill – Operations Manager

The softest hands in the Terminal

Besides having some 100s of grades of lub oil, there were many and varied grades of greases. The 'expert' here was Paddy 'Pa' Garrigan. Again a very good humoured man who always had a smile on his face. He filled 1 pound and 7 pound tins from bigger drums. He would scoop out the grease into the smaller tins, not with a ladle but with his hands and then using a stencil would put the grade name on each package ready for despatch. "No waste that way" he would say. 'Pa' claimed he had the softest hands in the terminal. It was said that 'Pa' could tell the grade and consistency of the grease where the name had disappeared from the container. Some say that he did this by taste!

Gerry Gilmore – Authorised Distributor Manager

A Regimented Business

To me, the Company was a very big change to working with a family run business. It was a very regimented business. There were rules to be kept and you kept them. I remember when I was appointed, the Personnel Manager, Bill Murdoch, calling me into his office and giving me advice, telling me all the things I should not do and also the things I should do. And I must say it was good advice. He said "You shouldn't be seen in the Shelbourne Hotel during certain hours, be in early in the morning and make sure there is spit and polish there all the time."

Basil Carr – Retail Promotions and Advertising Manager

Staying In

The Company changed a great deal in those years. Gradually, a few ladies were getting promotion. When I read the staff magazine Eolas now and see all these females with titles, well, we didn't have those kind of opportunities. Nobody got further than senior secretary and before I went there they used to have secretaries to the Assistant General Managers but they changed to central secretarial services or a typing pool as it was called then. So one person was put in charge of it and there again, there was a lot of dissension because people who had been secretaries were put into a typing pool which didn't suit them very well. Promotion was very slow for everybody because everybody stayed, once you got in you stayed.

Carmel Mallaghan – Secretary to Tom Crawford Young

Taking it to Heart

I remember a marvellous driver called Galvin we had on the Paraffin and TVO. He had his area sewn up. It was a very good agricultural area, around Clonakilty. The Equipment

Aladdin – Star of Stage and Home!

In 1960, the Christmas Pantomime at the Gaiety Theatre was sponsored by, who else but Aladdin Pink, Irish Shell's best-selling paraffin for domestic heaters. Our picture shows the pantomime stars, Jimmy O'Dea, Ursula Doyle, an unnamed Aladdin Representative and Maureen Potter in the Green Room of the Gaiety Theatre.

The smaller two photographs show the Pink Paraffin Delivery Service vans of T O'Callaghan of Shandon Street, Cork. Both photographs were taken in 1957 and that on the left shows the vans participating in the Cork St. Patrick's Day Parade on The South Mall.

manager came down and found his truck was in a terrible state. Anyway, the Equipment Manager tore a strip off your man. Well, he was a terribly sensitive fellow and he was almost crying. He told Bill O'Brien, the local superintendent, that he was chucking the job, and he started to walk for home which was in Kerry and the superintendent had to go after him in his car. He said he was fed up with Shell, he had done his best and he had marvellous sales. He took it to heart but eventually he was coaxed into changing his mind. Afterwards he became the Storekeeper.

William Moore – Government Relations

The Company Car

We worked Saturday mornings. We were given the use of a company car. My first was a dark blue Ford Anglia and you minded that with your life. You reported in every month the mileage you did and the mileage you incurred during personal use. You also were obliged to look for permission if you wanted to take the car outside your own territory.

Basil Carr – Retail Promotions and Advertising Manager

"And about Bloody Time..."

From Internal Auditor, I moved to Credit Manager, not the most sought-after job, but a good grounding – or should I say grinding – in sales staff/customer exhortation. It was during my term that Shell introduced Direct Debit, one of the first, if not the first company to introduce the practice into Ireland. It seemed unbelievably arrogant to ask customers "to hand over their chequebooks". *The bigger the company the easier it was to sell-in. I remember particularly, Leo Booth, subsequently managing director of the Smith Group. We became great friends later in my Retail life. After taking him painstakingly through the Direct Debit system, Tony O'Loughlin and myself were astounded by Leo's only comment* "And about bloody time" *and signed straight away.*

Perhaps even more spectacular, and encouraging, in those difficult days was the performance of Larry Hughes, our representative in the North Dublin area. The Rush Tomato growers, the canniest of canny farmers – were big business for Shell, we had practically the lot. Larry, in quick time, signed-up virtually them all He wasn't just a class act impersonating Hitler et al.

After Credit Manager, I took a brave step backwards into semi-seclusion to be appointed Retail Market Analyst. It was a totally new experience, not least the quarterly business meetings with Bernard Nolan and his back-up team of experts. One of these was Peter Murnaghan, a long-time friend and colleague until he died in service with BP. At one of my earlier meetings, I became embroiled with Bernard on some issue and was rapidly going up a blind alley. Peter attempted to rescue me, Bernard's hand went up stopping him in his tracks and I agonised to extract myself. It was a salutary lesson from Bernard and no better man to twist the bayonet which later I appreciated – know your facts before you open your big mouth!

Paddy Foley – Retail Services Manager

Scraggane – An Experiment in Self-help

Scraggane, an isolated fishing community jutting out into the Atlantic on the tip of the Dingle Peninsula, was the scene of an interesting rural self-help project backed by Irish Shell and BP in 1967. Under the guidance of Irish Shell and BP personnel, a badly-needed new slipway and access roads were built by the local community. Key company people involved in the project under the guidance of Managing Director Bernard Nolan were, (from left) Chris Hosford and Paddy Prendergast, who persuaded the local men to co-operate with the project, and Fred Schwab, who ran the project on site.

Pride in being a member of the Shell Team
There was great prestige in working for Shell and one took great pride in being a member of the Shell team. Shell were one of the few companies at the time who invested strongly in their brand other than in advertising and this came across in motorsport, racing and their association with the Ferrari team and with world rallying. You couldn't help but notice that Shell were the leaders in this area and consequently it gave the company some great prestige.

Basil Carr – Retail Promotions and Advertising Manager

Walter Joyce
Walter Joyce was a very nice man. He had been a major in the British Army and had been in the War. I think he had been in Shell before the War and he came back after it. When he retired he wrote a book about the history of his family, the Joyces of Galway. He had a big laugh which was very funny.

Carmel Mallaghan – Secretary to Tom Crawford Young

The Great Christy Ring
I knew Christy well and always made a point of trying to meet him at our Cork terminal when I went South. I found him a very shy, reserved man – as they say, "Backward at coming forward" – and not possessing the pushy, gregarious quality that one associates with a sales person. However, when Christy was promoted to a position as Sales Representative, he suited this job beyond all expectations. Nobody could refuse giving Christy an order.

I remember going out with Christy shortly after his new appointment and a typical scenario would be as follows. Going into, perhaps, a Co-op, Christy and myself would be ushered into the Manager's office, where the Manager might say, "That was a great game you played last Sunday, boy, you're still the Daddy of them all" and so the talk would proceed, going over every puck of the game.

With Christy saying very little, I would eventually nudge him and whisper something about an order. "An order, is it, Christy? Yerra, Bridie (the secretary), will you make out an order for Christy, whatever he wants".

Chris Hosford – Manager Southern Region Commercial

'Barney'
Noel Nunan brought Bernard Nolan into Shannon Airport once and Noel, because he played a bit of rugby, meet a number of his friends. Well, they kept referring to Nolan as 'Barney' and he was terribly annoyed, nobody ever called him Barney to his face. This was a time when you were always called by your surname, and you didn't mind because that was the time and everyone said 'Sir' to him. He was always 'Sir', he couldn't stick 'Barney' at all.

William Moore – Government Relations

Refuelling at Cork and Dublin Airports

Irish Shell and BP tankers engaged in refuelling an Aer Lingus Viscount at Cork Airport in the early 1960s.

The Shell and BP Aviation Service in operation refuelling an Aer Lingus Viscount at Dublin Airport in 1958.

Fore!

Jim Cosgrave, the 'Cosser' as he was affectionately known in the office, was the best story teller and mimic I have ever known. It was wonderful to listen to him when time allowed. However, it was fatal to ask him, say on a Monday morning as you arrived into the office, how he played at the weekend. You see, Jim was a good and keen golfer who played in the Island Golf Club. In recalling his game he might start with a description of the weather. It might have been blowing a gale or bitterly cold or a beautiful morning with the larks singing or whatever. It was important for him to set the scene. Then he was off and running. How he hit the drive down the first, followed by a "crisp" iron second and hit a right to left putt a bit too hard to take the break and so tapped in the short one for a four. This would continue for the 18 holes and his description of his shots together with the noise of each as the ball left the club – pssst and a pinggg – enthralled me but meant on some Mondays work started a little late until the round was over. Jim was a 'purist' and although the score was important I think it was the manner in which he compiled his score with those pinged drives and the crisp strike of his irons that gave him his greatest satisfaction.

Gerry Gilmore – Authorised Distributor Manager

The Mighty Christy Ring

Reproduced by
kind permission of
An Post ©

Of all the many sportsmen and women who were part of the Shell organisation in Ireland, no one would dispute the claim of Christy Ring to be the greatest of them all. No less than 8 All-Ireland medals were testament to the fact that this was the finest hurler ever to take the field, a fact acknowledged in 2000 when Christy was included in the An Post/GAA Team of the Millennium stamp series

Chapter 7

The 1970s:
De-merger and
Industrial Turmoil

A key document in ending the industrial unrest of the 1960s and 1970s, – the 1972 Irish Shell and BP Productivity Agreement.

1970-1979 Dublin Arms Trial – Parking meters introduced in Dublin – Decimal currency introduced – Direct dial to Belfast and London – OPEC Oil Crisis – Ireland joins the EEC – Inflation in Ireland at 20% – Northern Ireland's Executive collapses – Ireland joins the EMS – Wood Quay protests – Papal visit to Ireland – 60 mph speed limit introduced – Car safety becomes a major issue

The 1970s was an unsettled time in Irish history and as the decade progressed so it seemed that Irish Shell and BP was similarly affected by the mood of the times. Industrial unrest was the undercurrent of the decade and the company's 'on-off' relationship with BP finally ended in a divorce which was costly to both sides.

Before examining both these strands of the company's history, its worth looking for a few moments at how the company was progressing on other, perhaps more mundane, fronts but nevertheless important everyday operational issues which were all the time driving it forward and at the same time making it more recognisably the company we are familiar with today.

The decade began with the setting up of a Government Inquiry, the Fair Trade Commission's Inquiry into Motor Spirit Retail Outlets, established to investigate the nature and growth of petrol outlets. The Inquiry had come about mainly on account of pressure from the Petrol Retailers Association who were concerned by what they perceived as a multiplicity of outlets and a growing involvement of the petrol companies in the retail sector. Nine days of public hearings were held followed by a number of days of private hearings. During the course of the hearings, it was pointed out that a decade before the Inquiry, company-owned stations had accounted for 1% of the total of the total retail market. By 1969 that figure had grown to 26.7% and was still increasing.

As things turned out, it was to be early 1972 before the results of the 1970 Inquiry were published. The Commission in their report recognised that one of the previous measures proposed by them to curb the growth in retail outlets had encouraged the petrol companies to provide better security for their market share by concentrating on the development of company-owned sites rather than on privately-owned sites.

As a result of its deliberations, the Commission felt that only a limited number of new stations might be justified in the future to meet the needs created by new housing or road developments and it sought *"more positive financial and material assistance from the petrol companies"* to facilitate this development. At the same time the Commission increased the maximum permitted term of Solus agreements from five to ten years. An interesting statistic that emerged from the Report was that the petrol companies then controlled 31% of the national retail market, a figure rising to 58% in Dublin City and County.

Throughout the 1970s, operators of retail petrol sites agitated for greater security of tenure, the agreement under which they operated being a licence which was granted on a yearly basis. As a result the Irish Petrol Retailers Association was formed and one of the first things that it set out to do was to test this agreement in the courts. The test case occurred when a Shell retailer, John Costello, refused to resign his licence agreement when it was offered, leaving Shell with no option but to terminate the licence. The case was heard in the High court in Dublin before Justice Tommy Doyle and few could have imagined how long or tedious this test case would prove to be, some five years passing before judgement in favour of Irish Shell was given.

Against this backdrop, other Irish Shell and BP activities continued.

Life after Shell

Life does not end with retirement for Shell people and many have gone on to a second career or distinction in another field. Many are prominent in their local community; one such is John Lally who became a popular Mayor of his home town, Skerries, where he has also had a long and valued association with the annual Skerries Motor cycle races.

Gaelic Football Team – *c.* 1970

A Gaelic Football match was played against a team from Esso at St. Anne's Park, Raheny around 1970. This was the first Irish Shell Gaelic Football team to be formed. Its members were (back row from left): Unknown visitor, Tommy Payne, Pat Donoghue, Jim Brett, Pat Keogh, Dessie McCabe, Unknown, Hilary Allen, Shamie Connolly, John Gannon, Noel Murray, Paddy Melia. Front row (from left): Joe Tyrrell, Terry Tyrrell, Pat Browne, MIchael Coghlan, Shay McDonald, Michael Giles, Tommy Smith, Joe Reilly, Michael O'Malley and Seamus Bennett.

1970 saw the opening of a new facility at Dublin Airport, and a new Galway terminal was established. Road Safety became an increasingly important topic in Ireland and the company responded by introducing a Young Driver of the Year Award. The competition for the Award was open to all drivers between the ages of 17 and 25 holding a full unendorsed driving licence. No less than 400 entrants were selected to take part in the inaugural competition, first being examined in written tests held in Dublin, Cork, Limerick and Galway. The high scorers from each area were then graded on car handling, and finalists were selected to go forward to the national competitions in Dublin. The first winner was Ian McNeill of Dublin who was presented with his prize by Paudge Brennan TD, the Parliamentary Secretary to the Minister for Local Government. At the Awards presentation, Managing Director Bernard Nolan commented, *"Road safety has been a serious concern to our company for many years and we feel that the promotion of safe driving habits among young people is one of the most valuable investments we can make"*.

After a residency of almost 20 years, the company moved its headquarters from its long established offices at Fleet Street to No. 20 Hatch Street, Dublin, in 1970. The offices at Fleet Street had been outgrown and more importantly the need was felt to operate from a more modern facility better fitted to meet the needs of a modern business. The new office block at Hatch Street contained some 32,000 square feet of space and the latest design concepts were employed to provide a pleasant and highly adaptable work area. All staff were issued with a specially prepared booklet on the new building and the facilities in the area. The new building incorporated a fully equipped theatre and conference room and for the first time the company had a dedicated computer area. In a press release at the time, it was stated that:

> *The Computer Centre or area which includes the newly installed magnetic tape equipment is specially sealed to maintain the air-conditioned dust free environment required by this sensitive equipment. A glassed-in observation bay has been provided for visitors.*

In 1971, the new theatre was put to good use for the premier of a new Irish Shell film *The Little People* which had its first showing in the presence of An Taoiseach, Jack Lynch, and other members of the Government. The new film told the story of how, all over Ireland, often in remote, out of the way places, small factories and workshops were springing up, supported and assisted by

Hatch Street Headquarters

For almost 21 years, Shell House at Hatch Street, Dublin, served as the headquarters of Irish Shell, before the move in 1991 to the company's current base at Beech Hill Office Campus, Clonskeagh. No doubt there were times when it must have seemed like 'Hell House'!

State Sponsored bodies and design workshops. After the showing, An Taoiseach, Jack Lynch said of the film:

This film, which will be seen throughout the world, will go far to help to replace the image of the "Little People" of tradition with the "Little People" of reality who are doing so much to project an image of a modern Ireland and one of which we can be justly proud.

Made by Vincent Corcoran Productions with Vincent Corcoran also acting as cameraman, and with an entirely Irish crew, the film which was widely acclaimed was written by Irishman Tony Gray, and directed by Richard Taylor.

On the retail front, the 'Clean Sweep' nation-wide competition introduced in 1969 gathered momentum throughout the 1970s, having been introduced to improve site appearance and to raise the standards of service at both Shell and BP stations. As an indicator of its successful growth, the 1971 competition attracted no less than 300 entries. All 300 entries were visited by a panel of judges selected from the Motoring Press, the Advertising profession and Bord Fáilte, and points were awarded for cleanliness, tidiness, service, point-of-sale display and general site management. Cash prizes, as well as trophies were awarded to the winners.

Another safety initiative introduced was a very innovative concept aimed at instilling road sense in schoolchildren. This came about in 1972, when Irish Shell and BP presented Dublin Corporation with a fleet of pedal cars, bikes and road signs including miniature traffic lights to equip a new Traffic School which Dublin Corporation had built on a five acre site near Fairview Park in Dublin. This imaginative contribution to road safety in Ireland comprised a complete miniature road system with tarmacadamed carriageways, major and minor roads, roundabouts, one-way streets and pedestrian crossings. Children were, and indeed still are, for the Traffic School still operates today, taken in groups from schools to a classroom adjacent to the site where they are first given a period of instruction before proceeding out onto the traffic layout to participate in various educational traffic games. One look at the faces of the children using the Traffic School is confirmation that this is one of the best Road Safety initiatives ever undertaken in Ireland.

The 1973 Energy Crisis led to long queues at petrol pumps throughout the country but although supplies were short because of panic buying, the reality, as was pointed out by Bernard Nolan some time later, was quite

Shell Personalities in the 1960s and 1970s

Clockwise from top left: Vernon Goodchild, Company Secretary; John Farrell, Operations Manager who became Managing Director of BP Ireland after the de-merger; Niall O'Connell, Retail Manager and Herbie James, Operations Manager

different. Extravagant forecasts of the fall in demand for petrol were made, but in a market which was then growing annually by between 7 and 9 per cent, and in spite of a forty per cent increase in the pump price, demand dropped by only about 1½ per cent and was maintained during the duration of the crisis.

What did change, and change dramatically, was the operation of company owned sites. Following the sharp increase in the price of crude and the resultant effect on the price of petrol and therefore, motoring costs, service stations found it hard to make ends meet. No longer could the sale of petrol in itself sustain a living for the operator. Recession was biting hard and the public found it difficult to afford to service their cars. The established format of petrol pumps and service bay had to change and a way forward was beginning to appear on the High Street, where retailing was going through a major change. There, supermarkets had begun to make major inroads into the market and the corner shop was losing its position. To Shell this offered the opportunity to develop a new kind of service for their customers and the company began to seek permission for forecourt shops when redeveloping sites. In time, this would lead to today's revolution in the nature of petrol retailing and the development of the Select network of Convenience stores.

Whatever about the fulfilment of demand, the recession which accompanied the 1973 Energy Crisis put pressure on business and industry generally. Irish Shell and BP were not immune from this pressure and it was at least partly as a response to it that the de-merger of the two companies was announced in mid-1976. Speaking at the time of the announcement, Bernard Nolan stated:

> The most compelling (reason) is that, with the possible exception of South Africa, ours is the only country in the world where Shell and BP still market jointly. The circumstances which brought us together so long ago no longer obtain. The dramatic changes which the industry has undergone in the last few years reinforce the necessity for a break.

He continued:

> We see this reversion to independent marketing as an opportunity to renew the identity of both brands, (and) so develop divergent policies which will, no doubt, reflect the two companies different styles, philosophies, crude oil sources, refining abilities and so on which for so long have been compromised

The World Fishing Exhibition – 1971

The World Fishing Exhibition – the showroom of the world fishing industry – was held in Dublin in March 1971 at the RDS Showgrounds. Irish Shell and BP were represented with two stands – Shell Marine Services and BP Marine Services – which were staffed jointly by personnel from Irish Shell and BP and Shell-Mex and BP. Our photograph shows (from left): An Taoiseach, Jack Lynch; Aidan O'Carroll, Shell Lubricants – Irish Shell and BP; V E Thomas, Manager – Marine Department, and J P D Kierans, Shell-Mex and BP, on the Shell Marine Services Stand.

The Node

The Shell and BP Training Centre at The Node, Codicote, Herts., was a familiar venue to generations of Irish Shell personnel who attended training courses there.

165

within the Group. In future, each will have the opportunity to project a clear unambiguous image, sharply defined and strongly competitive. Each will be able to rely on the immense resources of its supplying company – resources which were important to us nationally two short years ago.

The de-merger took place on New Year's Day 1976 when BP Ireland took over the 500 service stations plus the aviation and bunkering business of British Petroleum in Ireland. The new Company – BP Ireland Limited – was headed by Longford-born solicitor, John C Farrell, who had been with Irish Shell and BP since 1958. BP Ireland Limited thus inherited a network selling just over 10% of the petrol in the Irish market and was expected to have a turnover in excess of £20 million annually. BP, while having its own delivery fleet, continued to draw product from the Shell terminals throughout the country. Around 80 ISBP staff transferred to the new company with the remaining 550 staying with Irish Shell which now reverted to the title, Irish Shell Limited.

It continued to supply the 700 Shell service stations (accounting for over 15% of the Irish petrol market) as well as the industrial, bitumen, commercial, domestic and agricultural markets. Irish Shell also supplied Shell Aviation fuel at the country's airports. The former Managing Director of Irish Shell and BP, Bernard Nolan, became Managing Director of Irish Shell Limited with Jim McStay as his Operations Manager. An interesting figure in the 1975 accounts of the company showed that the costs directly attributable to Irish Shell of the separation from BP were £155,000.

Industrial unrest came to the fore in the early 1970s, when various disputes with drivers and other operatives began to occur. One who was involved on behalf of Irish Shell in the negotiations with the unions was Des Murphy who recalled the long hours of negotiation and the inevitable aftermath:

When the strikes began to take place around 1972, I was involved in a lot of meetings at the FUE/PEA offices in Baggot Street and in the Labour Court. I can remember walking back along the canal with Pat Stephenson and Jim (McStay) and we'd be kind of rehearsing for what we would say to Bernard Nolan – it could take an hour to tell him everything that had been said with him being very critical. We had a lot of meetings at the Clarence Hotel. So many, in fact, that some smart-aleck pinched a plate from the hotel and presented it to me on my retirement!

Irish Shell and BP Productivity Agreement – 1972

The 1972 Productivity Agreement between Irish Shell and BP and the Irish Transport and General Workers' Union and the Amalgamated Union of Engineering Workers brought to an end a troubled period in the company's history. Pictured are some of those involved in the successful negotiations. From left in the top photograph: Jim Lee (Burmah Castrol); Tom Noonan (FUE); Dick Connolly (Conoco); John Fitzpatrick (BP); Andy Roche (FUE/PEA); John Doherty (FUE/PEA); Brendan Maher (Texaco); unknown; Jim McStay (Irish Shell); Des Murphy (Irish Shell) and Des Flood (Burmah Castrol).

Bottom photograph from left: Jim Lee (Burmah Castrol); Jim McStay and Des Murphy (Irish Shell); John Fitzpatrick (BP); unknown; Brendan Maher (Texaco) and Dick Connolly (Conoco).

As a result of these negotiations, the 1972 Irish Shell and BP Productivity Agreement came into being. In reality, its significance was that it paved the way for the transfer in later decades of a lot of the work then done by Irish Shell blue-collar workers to outside contractors, who were often ex-Irish Shell employees. This fundamental shift was an ongoing process throughout the 1970s and into the early 1980s and culminated in a drivers' strike in October 1980 which, although quickly ended, flared again in a more serious dispute in February 1981. The result was for the second time in the company's history, the deployment of the Defence Forces to ensure the distribution of essential petroleum products.

Shell Voices

Females didn't get very Far!
Bernard Nolan took over as Managing Director when Tom Young retired in 1964 and I worked for him until 1969. By then I was the most senior female in the Company. At that time females didn't get very far. But then job evaluations were introduced and everybody was being evaluated so when they came to do mine he said to me you really should have promotion. Now, the Finance Manager was always the Secretary of the Company and the Assistant Secretary was a man called Tom Oakes. Well, Tom Oakes retired and a man called Paddy Dunne was there. I was interested in the personnel side of things and had worked with them very closely because in my position in Tom Young's office I did all the salaries of the managers and year-end increases were all done by himself and myself together. Anyway, Paddy Dunne decided to leave and went to the Industrial Development Authority so I got his job. That was a big change for me. I worked with the solicitor who at the time was Tom O'Donoghue. It was very interesting and I was glad to be in work where I could use my qualification so I remained there until 1982.

Carmel Mallaghan – Secretary to Tom Crawford Young

Bearding the Lion in his Den
I received a telephone call early one frosty Saturday morning, telling me that one of our lorries, en route from Dublin terminal to our Kells depot had skidded approaching the new bridge across the River Boyne, a few miles on the Dublin side of Navan. I hurried to the scene. The vehicle had crashed through the iron railings of the bridge, had fallen about 20 feet down an embankment and was partially submerged on its side. It contained diesel oil, a deadly substance to be loosed on a lovely river. I could see that although the vehicle was badly damaged, the tank compartments were not leaking badly. My first thought was the driver, whom the numerous onlookers told me had been taken to the local hospital. Visiting him, I was delighted to find that apart from some scratches and being badly shaken, he was all right. Coming back to the scene of the accident, I could see that the leak was causing a

The Shell Puissance

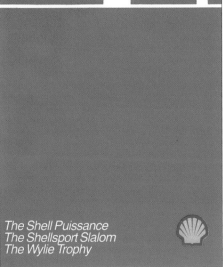

During the late 1970s and the early 1980s, The Shell Puissance was one of the highlights of the Dublin Horse Show at the Royal Dublin Society's grounds at Ballsbridge. The Puissance, and the Shellsport Slalom, run on the same day, always attracted a top-class entry and were won by several of the top names in Showjumping, including the redoubtable Harvey Smith who was the 1982 winner on 'Sanyo Olympic Video', and who is here seen being congratulated by Irish Shell Managing Director, Bernard Nolan.

thin film of oil to drift down the river, on top of the surface. I was approached by some highly incensed local anglers who told me that this could mean the total destruction of fish life – salmon and trout – on one of the finest fishing rivers in Leinster. I was further informed that I had better report the accident to a titled gentleman, who was chairman of the Boyne Fishing Conservancy, or some appellation like this. I was informed that he was a very fiery individual and that he would "have my guts for garters", and that the incident could well cost the Shell company millions of pounds if the fishing was interfered with. I decided to "Beard the lion in his den", but before doing so I did a quick survey of the river immediately below the bridge. I noticed the remains of a mill stream or canal in the vicinity of the town of Navan. I devised a plan to construct a barrier down-river and with this in mind I drove into Navan, contacted as many builders as I could find, instructed them to lay their hands on as many timber planks as they could and directed them to lay out these timbers across the Boyne, diagonally, so that the film of oil could be trapped and diverted into the old waterway. I then set off, with my heart in my shoes, to meet the 'Monster'. When I called to his house I explained what had happened and the steps I was taking to alleviate the dangerous situation. To my amazement, he turned out to be most compassionate. He could see I was visibly shaken. He poured out a large glass of brandy for me, awoke his two sons who were home on holiday from Eton College and who were sleeping late after a party the previous night and instructed them to come back with me and render whatever help they could.

I ordered a heavy duty crane from Dublin, an empty lorry and pumping equipment and by late evening, I had the oil pumped out of the stricken vehicle into the tanks of the lorry on the road. The crane was then able to lift the empty vehicle back onto the highway. The contamination caused by the leaked oil was minimal but I shudder to think of the consequences if all the tank compartments on the lorry had been ruptured and the entire load of diesel oil discharged into the river.

Gerry O'Neill – Operations Manager

You ought to be ashamed of yourself!

There was an occasion when Barney Nolan went down to Cork wearing his customary anorak and was addressing the yard staff who were of course all dressed in anoraks as well. So one fellow stood up and said "With all due respects, Mr Nolan, you might have put on a f****** suit when you were coming to address us and not be dressed in that yoke!" *He said,* "I wear this all the time". "Well, you ought to be ashamed of yourself!"

Jack Dunne – Pensioners Liaision Representative

The 42.5% Increase!

I joined Shell in 1972 and I was interviewed by B A Nolan, Vernon Goodchild and Frank Rich who was then the legal advisor for Shell UK. The interview went well until it came to the question of remuneration. When asked what salary I was expecting, I decided to be brave and demand an increase of £250 over my then salary of £2,000. I thought this reasonable in view of the fact that I was changing jobs. However, I was astonished when I received an

Donegal Oil Company

The Board of Directors of Donegal Oil Company photographed in 1979 when the company was celebrating 25 years as a Shell AD. Seated is A E McMahon while those standing are (from left): Jim Kennedy, S D MacLoughlainn, Derek McMahon and Michael Geary.
The other photographs are (clockwise from top left): The old Shell Depot at Letterkenny in 1951; Donegal Oil Company staff and friends at their Annual Dinner dance at Rathmullan in December 1968; A view of the Letterkenny Depot c.1979; Driver Charlie Moore with Tanker and Trailer c.1958.

171

offer of the job at £2,750 and not only that but after starting on January 1st, the National Wage Agreement of the day kicked in with a further increase of £100. There was no doubt that I saw a future in a company who were prepared to hand over increases of 42.5%!

Declan Fallon – Corporate Services Manager

Social and Sporting Activities

There was an annual outing in the Summer, when employees participated in various sporting events, tennis, golf, fishing etc. I helped to get a boating section organised with Paddy Walsh and the late Cecil Buggy and we purchased a small motorboat which we moored in the Coal Harbour in Dún Laoghaire. We had many a pleasant evening fishing off Dalkey and the Muglins and we sometimes ventured further to Bray and across the way to Howth.

I cannot speak highly enough of the committee in Dublin Terminal who raised funds and organised an annual Christmas Party, which was held each year on a Sunday afternoon just before Christmas in the CIE Club in Marlborough Street. It was a delight to see hundreds of employees' happy children enjoying themselves at this function. Some of the funds collected were devoted to the organisation of another children's Christmas Party at the orphanage in Dún Laoghaire which the good Sisters in charge enjoyed as much as the children. There was also the annual Soccer challenge match against a team from SM&BP in Northern Ireland. We played the match alternately in Belfast and Dublin. I, myself, participated in this event, even though I was then beyond my 'sell-by' date.

Gerry O'Neill – Operations Manager

The Prince of Waggishness

During the early 1970s, a certain product manager (who was short-sighted even when wearing his bottle-end specs) bustled into the office (Lower Hatch Street) for an early morning meeting with the Ad. agency. As it was a large open-plan layout, desks and bodies seemed to breed in an unbridled fashion. In his rush to pick up his papers, he banged into the corner of a desk and sustained a bad bruising to his knee, calling down at the same time various torments on the culpable. The late Wally Scott – who was a prince of waggishness – enquired of the afflicted manager, "What happened to your glasses?" *The distressed manager replied,* "Mary stood on them this morning in the bedroom." *To which Wally replied in baffled seriousness,* "Were you wearing them at the time?"

Noel Tierney – Public Affairs Manager

"Perfidious Albion!"

I remember a meeting in London with Shell UK when we were an independent supplier and they were trying to charge us prices which were inappropriate. Now, when Bernard Nolan believed in you, he really backed you. He sat across the table from these very senior Shell executives and said "Perfidious Albion, you know where the name came from, and why, and it was well deserved." *Well, I wanted to slide under the table and get out of the room. There was a stony silence but he made his point.*

Gerry McManus – Marketing Manager, Director

Terry Balfe and Irish Motorsport

In the 1960s and '70s, Terry Balfe was responsible for Irish Shell's extensive involvement in Irish motorsport. The Shell tankers were a familiar sight at events throughout the country and most especially, as in these photographs, at the 'Park' – the annual Irish Motor Racing Club races in Dublin's Phoenix Park. Shown dispensing Shell product are (from left): Paddy Kennedy, Terry Balfe and Bert Crosland.

173

Chapter 8

The 1980s:
New Beginnings

Shell Super Multigrade was heavily promoted, particularly through motor sport throughout the 1980s.

1980-1989 PAYE Marches – Garrett Fitzgerald becomes Taoiseach – Stardust tragedy – Petrol crisis – Ireland wins Triple Crown in 1982 and 1985 – IRA Hunger Strikes – Car Assembly ends – Bob Geldof organises Live Aid – Falklands War – Stephen Roche wins Tour de France – Hillsborough Agreement

The 1980s began with yet another Government Inquiry into aspects of the oil industry. On this occasion the Inquiry arose from complaints from the Irish Petrol Retailers Association who claimed that the conditions under which petrol sites were leased were unfair in that the retailer was neither tenant or employee and as a result was not protected under the Landlord and Tenant, Employment or Social Welfare legislation. After an eighteen day hearing, the Inquiry recognised the validity of the Agreement but extended its term to three years. Additionally, conditions were introduced which allowed the Agreement to be terminated during its term as well as allowing the concept of 'rollover'. Another important change was the dropping of the limitation on the expansion of company owned networks.

Shortly afterwards, it was announced that Bernard Nolan would be retiring from the role of Managing Director which he had held since 1964.

Bernard Nolan was succeeded by James M Beveridge who had been head of Marketing Distribution Development in Shell International Petroleum since 1975. Jim Beveridge had joined the Shell Group in 1951 after graduating from University College, Dublin, and had held marketing appointments in the Far East, Africa, the Caribbean and Europe, where he was General Manager in Switzerland. He later served in the Shell International Service Companies in The Hague and in London.

Taking up his appointment in August of 1981, Jim Beveridge found Irish Shell facing some tough decisions. The serious nature of these decisions was highlighted by the 1982 Company Report when, in June, he announced a loss of £14.5 million in the preceding year. In a hard-hitting review of the Company's operations, Jim Beveridge singled out *"the tardy operation"* of the price-control mechanism imposed by the Government on the Oil Industry, as the major factor in the loss – some £9.5 million having been caused by this single factor. Other factors which pushed up costs were the *"expensive"* intervention by the Government in the settlement with oil tanker drivers during the strikes of October 1980 and February 1981. The difficulties were added to by the operation and subsequent maintenance on stand-by of uneconomic refining capacity at Whitegate. What was already going to be a difficult year was made even more difficult by the Government's requirement that Irish Shell and its competitors maintain stocks at levels which were far in excess of operating needs in order to comply with EEC regulations relating to compulsory stock. Jim Beveridge, at the time, pointed out:

> *This requirement of providing the national strategic reserve, inequitably controlled as it is, goes unremunerated in any way – a situation almost unique amongst the EEC countries and particularly onerous in periods of high interest rates.*

Sadly, the result of all this was a necessity to trim the labour force by about one-fifth and as a result around 100 redundancies were planned. In fact, it was not until 1983 that the Company returned to profit after two years of serious losses, the Report and Accounts for the year ending 1983 showing a profit of £1.9 million on gross sales of £320 million. This period was made particularly difficult for all concerned by what was perceived to be a total inability or desire on the part of the Government of the day to understand the Oil companies difficulties. In particular the operation of the price-control mechanism was disastrous and added greatly to the loss at Irish Shell.

James M Beveridge

Jim Beveridge succeeded Bernard Nolan as Managing Director in August 1981. Previously head of Marketing Distribution Development in Shell International Petroleum, Jim had joined the Shell Group in 1951 after graduating from University College, Dublin. Jim had held marketing appointments in the Far East, Africa, the Caribbean and Europe, where he was General Manager in Switzerland. He also served in the Shell International Companies in The Hague and in London.

Things were also changing on other fronts – in particular, with relation to Irish Shell's position within the Shell 'family'. Prior to the early eighties, those within Irish Shell had a tendency to view the company as a Branch rather than as a Company in its own right. This undoubtedly was a result of the arrangements that had existed between the British and Irish companies in the 1920s and 1930s, but had long since ceased to have any meaning in reality. As a result of new attitudes, Irish Shell now began to look towards Europe and to take its place – however belatedly – within the European Shell family.

Change was also in the air for another important aspect of Shell's business in Ireland; its bitumen interests. Since the early 1950s, bitumen had made a significant contribution to Shell profits, and the Colas company was essentially the downstream end of the bitumen business where products such as bitumen emulsion and jointing compounds were manufactured using bitumen as their raw material. Colas companies existed not just in the Irish market but also in the UK and around Europe with all having a common trade name derived from 'coal asphalt', hence Colas. In Britain these companies were owned by the Shell operating company, but in Ireland their ownership was in the hands of private individuals with Shell having a shareholding. Thus in Ireland, the biggest private operator was Cold Chon owned by the Coyle family in Galway, who had set up the company in the 1920s using the name 'CHON' which came from the first letters of each of the constituents of Bitumen; 'C' for carbon, 'H' for hydrogen, 'O' for oxygen, and 'N' for nitrogen.

Now, in the early 1980s, Shell began to buy out all these minority shareholders. Amongst them were two companies based in Dublin – Colfix and a company which had been separated out to deal with building products as opposed to road products. This company was Shell Composites. Patrick Lynch joined Colas around this time with a brief to consolidate all of these companies into a cohesive unit that would trade and report into Shell on a consolidated basis. However, this was into Shell UK which owned the shareholding in the Colas companies in Ireland, an arrangement which remained in place until the early 1990s when Irish Shell became the shareholder in these companies.

Another small but significant part of the change of direction within Irish Shell, was the introduction of Eolas – *"A Newsletter for Shell Staff in Ireland"*. The idea of Jim Beveridge and with a particularly appropriate title, Ruth McDonnell became its first Editor and Eolas quickly became an important communication tool as well as serving to bring staff together

Eólas

Eólas – "The Newsletter for Shell Staff in Ireland" came into being during the stewardship of Managing Director Jim Beveridge in Autumn 1982 and has proved to be an important means of providing information and communication to staff past and present. The inaugural issue is illustrated below (left) as well as the current format (above right) and an 1986 issue (below right). During its lifespan, Eólas has had a number of Editors, the first being Ruth McDonnell, followed by Nuala Moore, Zoë Devlin and Annette Martin.

during a difficult time for the company. Subsequent Editors of Eolas have included Nuala Moore, Zoë Devlin and Annette Martin.

In 1983, the company celebrated 75 years of Service in Ireland. (This date was based on the purchase of the Dublin Installation site at Alexandra Road and not on Shell's earliest involvement in Ireland which occured in 1902). The celebrations were an important means also of throwing off the dark clouds which had surrounded the company during the preceding few years of losses and consequent change and celebratory dinners and other special events were held throughout the country. One of the special events was an Exhibition of Shell Advertising Art held at the National Concert Hall in Dublin and subsequently at a number of other venues throughout the country.

In June 1984, Lord Killanin retired from the Board of Irish Shell. Distinguished in several fields, Lord Killanin had joined the Board in 1946, thus serving for 38 years, by far the longest service of any non-executive director.

The following November, Austrian racing driver, Niki Lauda, who had just won his third F1 Drivers World Championship title, piloted his own plane into Dublin to launch Shell's 'Shell Sport '85' – an ambitious programme of sporting involvement for the Irish company. Lauda, whose airline, Lauda Air, was then in the midst of a bitter dispute with the Austrian Government over routes, spent every free minute of his Dublin visit on the phone to his representatives in Austria. That is not to say that he neglected his duties in Dublin and a most exacting schedule of appearances together with the obligatory round of media interviews was completed before the extraordinary Herr Lauda left Dublin later the same evening.

The list of events contained within the Shell Sport '85 programme is particularly interesting and gives an excellent indication of the depth of the Company's involvement at that time in Irish sporting and cultural life. Not surprisingly, given the importance that Shell places on it world-wide, motor sport was to the fore. John Rowe, the Company's Marketing Director, announced Irish Shell's exclusive sponsorship of the Dealer Opel Team Ireland Manta 400 to be driven by Austin McHale and Christy Farrell in the STP Tarmac Rally Championship. At the same time, the Company continued its long-term association with Ireland's top rally driver, Billy Coleman of Millstreet. Coleman, who had achieved a clean sweep of the Irish International rallies in 1984, was to carry personal support from Irish Shell, while driving for his new team, Rothmans' Porsche. In addition, Irish Shell sponsored the National Rally Championship which it saw as an important

Lord Killanin

Irish Shell's longest serving non-executive director, Lord Killanin, first became a director in 1946, a role in which he continued until his retirement in 1984 – a period of 38 years. A man of many talents, Lord Killanin is best remembered as head of the Olympic movement during a particularly difficult time in its history, through which he guided it with a sure hand and not a little style.

stepping stone for up and coming talent. Finally on the rally front, Irish Shell continued to support, in association with its local distributors, Donegal Oil Company and Inishowen Oil Company, the Donegal International Rally. Other motor sport events to receive Shell support in 1985 were: The Skerries Motor Cycle Races; The M G Car Club Economy Run; The Formula Ford 'B' Championship at Mondello; the Phoenix Park Races and the Circuit of Ireland Rally.

Turning away from motor sport, Irish Shell sponsored the Shell Advertising Art Exhibition at Waterford; Junior Chamber Ireland's 'Living with Leisure' Exhibition; The Inland Waterways Association; The Army Apprentices School Awards; The National Institute of Higher Education Dublin Scholarship for Students of Languages and the International Marketing Course; The Irish Youth Choir; the Rathmines & Rathgar Musical Society; Dublin Corporation's Traffic School at Clontarf; Show jumping at the Royal Dublin Society's Horse Show and the Irish International Ballet. Finally, Irish Shell was patron to Macra na Feirme; The Dublin Grand Opera Society; The Team Theatre Group and Dublin Zoo – an association of long-standing. Covenants were bestowed upon Trinity College, Dublin; The Heritage Trust and the Eye and Ear Hospital, Dublin.

A fondly remembered event from this time is the Irish Shell Hobbies and Crafts Exhibition which was held in December 1985. A total of 101 entries to a very high standard were received ranging from oil paintings to restored antique furniture.

An instrument of considerable change, Jim Beveridge's tenure as Managing Director of Irish Shell was to be quite short and in 1986, upon his retirement, John Withrington was appointed to succeed him. A native of Cork, John Withrington had joined the Shell Group in 1969, having graduated in engineering at Trinity College, Dublin. He also completed a doctorate at Oxford. Within the Shell Group, he held appointments in London and Houston before coming to Ireland.

The re-introduction of Price Controls by the Minister for Industry and Commerce, in the Autumn of 1987 brought a new challenge to the company. These dramatic times are recalled by John Withrington:

In 1989 Ray Burke was Minister for Industry and Commerce. Oil prices were rising and the Government became very worried about inflation. There was a Cabinet decision to freeze oil prices. Ray Burke announced this and then went off on a trip to Japan to promote Ireland in the Far East. Within days of his having announced this freeze we were into negative margins territory and I

182

The Shell Advertising Art
Exhibition – 1983

An Exhibition of Shell Advertising Art was opened at the National Concert hall, Dublin, in December 1983. In the photograph is Managing Director, Jim Beveridge, showing a Shell Lorry Poster dating from 1925 to Ruairi Quinn TD. The poster portrays Killarney's Devil's Island and was one of a series of scenic beauty spots in Ireland. At top is the cover of the Catalogue produced by Irish Shell for the exhibition which also travelled to several other locations throughout Ireland.

wrote to Haughey, who was Taoiseach at the time, saying we urgently needed a meeting and explaining that we could not continue to sell at a lower price than we could buy on the open market. I got a message back to say we would have to wait for a meeting until Ray Burke returned in due course. As a result, we announced that we would continue to supply the market from stock but we could not justify buying product at prices which exceeded what we were allowed to sell it at. I knew there would be a reaction but I had no idea how much. We were the first item on the news the whole week because Shell was the one to lead on this and some others followed and some didn't. I remember being very pleased that some of the other oil companies followed our lead. So, we had varying degrees of solidarity on this issue but Shell's name was at the fore. At first, the Government was extremely angry because they thought we were holding them to ransom but I pointed out that we had told them we had needed an urgent meeting which they had refused to have and that I had no mandate to sell at a price less than we bought. Eventually, a compromise proposal was devised which allowed the matter to be resolved to our satisfaction.

As a result, an Inquiry was set-up by the Government which opened in May and came to an end after two months of hearings. The Restrictive Practices Inquiry, as the group was titled, issued an interim report vindicating the position taken by Irish Shell at the Inquiry, recommending the removal of price controls and the introduction of price display signs at retail sites.

The resolution of this difficulty and the establishment of a more realistic cost-base for the company's continuing operations in Ireland were to form the major accomplishments of John Withrington's time as Managing Director of Irish Shell.

The company resumed its role as an innovator in the Irish market with the launch of Unleaded petrol in September 1987 with a small ceremony at the East Link Service Station in Dublin, which was attended by the Minister for the Environment, Pádraig Flynn TD. A series of bold marketing initiatives by Irish Shell over the next several years helped to rapidly develop the market for Unleaded fuels in Ireland – a market in which today Shell remains both an innovator and market leader.

Petrol was in the news again the following spring, when Irish Shell withdrew its Formula Shell petrol from the Irish market. Formula Shell had been introduced the previous year onto the Irish market and was on sale in 33 countries around the world. The unique properties of Formula Shell were an advanced detergent which cleaned the combustion chamber of the

John Withrington

In 1986, John Withrington was appointed to replace Jim Beveridge as Managing Director. A native of Cork, John Withrington had joined the Shell Group in 1969, having graduated in engineering at Trinity College, Dublin. Before coming to Ireland, he held appointments within the Shell Group in London and Houston.

engine and a potassium-based spark-aider which resulted in improved combustion and therefore greater fuel efficiency. Shell had been working with potassium as a spark-aiding additive for many years but it was only during the development of Formula Shell that its researchers were able to harness its special properties to give measurable performance improvements in motor vehicles. A massive testing programme involving more than 400 vehicles driving more than 6 million kilometres in several different countries and in varying climates was undertaken prior to the launch of the brand. The testing produced evidence of the benefits of Formula Shell in drivability, fuel economy and emissions. It did not reveal any problems.

Subsequently, problems arose in Norway and Denmark with a very small proportion of vehicles that used Formula Shell encountering an increased incidence of valve burning. While the number of incidents was statistically very small, the company was concerned about marketplace perceptions of the brand. No problems whatsoever were found with the product in Ireland, but Irish Shell took the decision to withdraw it from the market. Gerry McManus, Marketing Director of Irish Shell commented:

> We were all very disappointed at how events turned out. It was an extremely successful marketing initiative, but unfortunately it was not possible to continue to promote and market Formula Shell in Ireland when our nearest neighbour withdrew. The Shell brand is synonymous with quality and there can be no reason for even the slightest perception of doubt about any of our products.

Although Formula Shell had proven to be a false start, further motor fuel innovations followed over the next two years with the introduction of Shell Super Plus Unleaded and Shell Advanced, both of which were to prove successful in the marketplace.

Shell Voices

The 'Isis'
On the Shell Outing in June 1981, the Isis broke down and we were towed in from Scotsman's Bay by the Dún Laoghaire lifeboat. Needless to say, it was a big laugh to all at the Shell dinner that night.

Larry Hughes – Commercial Representative

A Unique and Special Occasion

Four generations of Managing Director were photographed together in 1986. They are from left: Tom Crawford Young (Managing Director from 1948 – 1964); Bernard Nolan (1964-1981); Jim Beveridge (1981-1986) and John Withrington (1986-1990).

The First Restrictive Practices Enquiry

The public sitting was held in the old Land Commission offices in Merrion Square where the Merrion Hotel now stands. The Enquiry opened on a very hot July day in a room which was far too small for the number of legal luminaries and clients who had gathered for the start of the hearings. The heat was overbearing despite all the windows being opened. It was amusing to watch some of the leading Senior Council of the day scrambling to get a seat in the front row. They were in direct conflict with their oil company clients who also felt they should be in the front row. However, order was soon restored with the clients being relegated to the back rows.

Declan Fallon, Public Affairs Manager

Work-to-rule

Blue collar meeting in Lower Hatch Street in the early eighties. Three union officials, twelve shop stewards and six management engaged in heated debate across the table. Agreement was nowhere near and one shop steward stated "We're not making any progress on our claim and therefore we intend to implement a work-to-rule with immediate effect." *There was silence in the room for a few moments and then the Operations Manager asked* "How will we know?"

Willie Barry – Human Resources Manager

Final Years

My final appointment before retiring in 1984 at 55 years was Retail Services Manager wherein I worked under a number of Retail Managers. Niall O'Connell was a gentleman; and Frank McArdle, whose roar was truly worse than his bite . I remember Dick Longfield returning regularly, haggard and dismayed, from another coffee-morning-mauling from Bernard. And finally Matt Langan who successfully held off some of Jim Beveridge's bewildering torrent of ideas for better retail marketing and who saw me finally out the door.

Paddy Foley – Retail Services Manager

The Top Floor Wine Lake

White collar Union meeting at Lower Hatch Street in the mid-eighties. Lunch was taken around the negotiating table. One of the water jugs was empty and the Union Branch Secretary said "Any chance of someone going up to the 'wine lake' on the top floor and filling the jug?"

Willie Barry – Human Resources Manager

The Lights are Out...

Jim Beveridge was addressing drivers in Cork about forthcoming changes and the initial part of upcoming redundancies. He was getting at best, I think, an indifferent response and was pacing up and down the room as he listened. The room had been darkened for slides and Jim suddenly pulled back the curtains and looked out. He stood looking for a few moments and then said to the driver who was nearest to him, "What are those buildings there?"

The Shell Shannon Guides

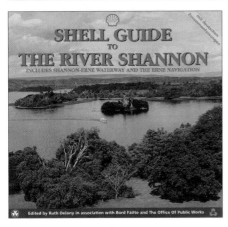

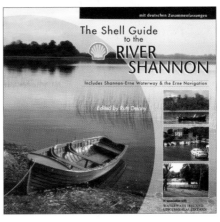

Appropriately for a company with so many links to the river, Irish Shell has, down the years, produced a series of guides to navigation on the River Shannon as well as to the river itself and its environs – a few of which are illustrated here. These Shell guides have become essential to all those who travel the river – for business or, as is more often the case today, for pleasure.

189

The reply came back "That's Ford and that's Dunlops". Jim said "You notice the lights are out on both of them". *After another few moments pause, he said* "Now, lets get back to our discussions".

Jack Dunne, Marketing Services Manager

Jim Beveridge
I think Jim brought a tremendous panache to the company. I think that he re-instilled a self-confidence into the company. Jim had the grand gesture, the self-confidence. He had also a lot of credibility within Shell. He put a huge amount of capital into the company at a time when it was also seen that the company was over-manned and I think its a very difficult message to get across that you need a lot more investment but by the way, we want to get rid of more people. It was true, but a very difficult message to get across and it was my perception that he had a very rough time with the Unions.

John Withrington – Managing Director 1986-1990

Ronald Reagan's Radio Commercial
Sometime during the 1980s, a radio ad was produced by our advertising agency, Momentum, using the intonation of Ronnie Reagan. I think it was done by Jonathan Ryan; his voice portrayal was superb, even down to the vapid chortle.

From the first day it went on air, we came under fire, strangely not from the public but from one unnerved director. At the time, most of the oil majors ads over this period could be said to be reasonably good, if not inspiring. To break custom it was decided to distinguish itself from the undeviating mediocrity of the common herd – the other oil majors. As Ronald Reagan was in the news everyday – Thatcher and the Atlantic Friendship Pact, Gorby and the removal of Cruise missiles from Europe, Ollie North and Irangate, not forgetting Ron's capacity for blunders when he abandoned his minders or the auto-cue – the ad reflected his foibles and was delivered in the inimitable voice of Ronald Reagan, ably impersonated by Jonathan Ryan.

Such was the internal pressure to remove the ad that we had to do so within two days!

Noel Tierney – Public Affairs Manager

(Author's note: I have particularly good reason to remember this advertisement as I was managing director of Momentum when it was produced. I recall a meeting to decide its fate held at Irish Shell and being horrified upon my return to the office to discover that the copywriter who had originated the advertisement had taken it upon himself to bring it down to the American Embassy for a second opinion. I need not have worried. Upon playing it to a group of officials at the Embassy, their reaction was to fall around the floor laughing. In short, they loved it but didn't think we should use it. Exit one disappointed copywriter but not before he had promised to supply several copies of the tape to the audience for their own amusement!)

F1 and Grass-Roots – Shell in Motorsport

The Irish Shell Economy Run organised each year by the MG Car Club is the longest running continuous sporting event with which Irish Shell is associated. To mark its 30th anniversary in 1993, past winners of the event gathered to compete for a 'Past Masters Trophy'. These included: (from left) Paul Phelan, Fred Connor, Des Bradley, John Tansey, Nigel Jones, John Horan, Matt O'Grady and John Ryan.

Eddie Irvine – Ferrari F1 Driver

In 1996, Shell International renewed its partnership with the Ferrari Formula One team. The inclusion of Northern Ireland driver, Eddie Irvine, in the team's driver line-up provided an additional reason for Irish Shell to capitalise on this significant sponsorship. To date, no less than 20 Drivers and 14 Constructors titles have been won using Shell products.

Job Lot
I never applied to join Irish Shell. I had been working in Ergas for about 10 years. Then, Irish Shell bought the company and got me as part of a 'job lot'.

Michael Forde – Managing Director, 1996-2001

Bad Relationships
There was a rosy period in 1986 when the company was making money and this was due to 'happy circumstances' with oil prices coming down but we were really hit in late '86 and early '87 and the thing that really put pressure on us was Albert Reynolds introducing Price Controls. Albert Reynolds was the Minister for Industry and Commerce and he arbitrarily imposed a price cut which had a really significant effect on our profitability. I remember going to see Albert Reynolds with Gerry McManus. This was the first time I had met him and I realised the extreme hostility with which the oil industry was viewed. I explained what I thought the situation was and he said to me "Why should I give in to you?" And I thought is the relationship so bad that he's calling me a liar? So, that set me back because I realised that the oil industry as a whole had an extremely bad reputation and not only had it a bad reputation, but a bad relationship with Government. While I was extremely upset about what he did, I think looking back on it that it was a crude measure but maybe it was a necessary measure because when I began to really understand the cost structure I realised that we had inherited throught the various strikes a cost structure which was totally unsustainable.

John Withrington – Managing Director 1986-1990

The 'Bugs' Company
Shortly after I came into Irish Shell, there was a big push from the UK to get involved in businesses outside the traditional oil sector. As a result, the International Biochemical Group, whose business was the development and sale of microbiological solutions for waste treatment, was targeted for acquisition. I was very much involved in the team which made the acquisition in 1985. I then went to the UK from 1986 to 1989. On my return, we had a visit from a big chief – one of the Committee of Managing Directors – who decided that IBG had no future. So, I spent a large part of 1990 selling the company.

Michael Forde – Managing Director 1996-2001

The Structure of Change in the 1980s
The major achievement of the 1980s was that Irish Shell for the last 4-5 years clearly established itself as a viable operating company in its own right. This was achieved through a lot of things and one person to whom I give a lot of credit for that was Bob Reid (and later Sir Bob Reid, Chairman of Shell UK) who at a time when the shareholders and people in Shell UK were questioning our ability to manage our own affairs, said "What do you want to do?" And having heard, he said "Well, do it." At that time we were being asked to withdraw, or it was being suggested that we should withdraw from certain markets as we couldn't make a living from them. Fuel oil in particular and from certain geographic areas. Arising from that, we said that we would stay in any market where we could be viable – that

192

Air Spectacular 1993

Irish Shell has had a long association with the Irish Army Air
Corps and has been pleased to be a patron of several 'Air
Spectaculars'. One of the highlights of these memorable occasions
has been the performance of the Air Corp's own 'Silver Swallows'
Display Team flying their graceful Fouga Magister aircraft.
The 'Silver Swallows' team – now sadly no more – received
international acclaim for their displays and were highly regarded
by their fellow display pilots of other air forces.

was our own internal policy so the structure of change that happened in the 1980s was centred around making ourselves viable in as many markets as we could. As it turned out we had to close terminals but we stayed in the markets.

Jim Beveridge and John Withrington were both overseers of this change. Neither was the catalyst for the change – that came as much internally as from outside.

Gerry McManus – Marketing Manager, Director

Chapter 9

The 1990s and Beyond: A Good Neighbour

The latest Shell logo in a long process of evolution was introduced in 1995.

1990-2001 Irish success in Italia '90 – The Gulf War – Mary Robinson becomes President of the Republic of Ireland – Death of Princess Diana – The Celtic Tiger – The Good Friday Agreement – The Omagh Bombing – Millennium Celebrations

Future historians of industry are likely to recognise in the decade of the 1990s the start of a new era of increased scrutiny for the operations of multi-nationals. No longer could an insular view be taken by management of the operations of Irish Shell, for, as the company was soon to discover, it could be, and indeed was, increasingly identified with the actions of other Shell companies in other geographic locations. For this reason, Irish Shell has been forced to take an increasingly global view of its operations and, as a consequence, reflecting this development, the attention given to the company's Public Affairs function grew dramatically as the decade advanced.

One early effect of this was that it became essential for Irish Shell to attain internationally acknowledged standards of operation and following assessment by the National Standards Authority of Ireland, the company received, in July 1991, the prestigious IS/ISO 9002/EN29002 Award embracing the complete range of activities it carries on in Ireland – purchase, storage, blending and distribution of hydrocarbon fuels and lubricants. The Certificate was presented to the company at a ceremony in the following September by Robert Molloy TD, Minister for Energy.

Before this happened, however, John Withrington, who had been Managing Director of the company since 1986, left to take up a senior appointment in the Middle-East Regional Organisation of Shell International Petroleum Company Limited in London. John was succeeded by Patrick Lynch, a native of Galway, who had joined the Shell Group as Managing Director of Colas Group of companies in Ireland in 1982 and who since 1985 had held appointments with Shell International Petroleum Company and Shell (UK) in London.

The Shell Emergency Plan was put to the test in February 1990, when the mv *Tribulus*, a bulk ore carrier owned by Shell Tankers got into difficulty some 260 miles off the South West coast of Ireland. Irish Shell assisted the Shell Tankers UK Emergency Response Team in the difficult task of first ensuring the safety of the crew and then bringing the *Tribulus* to a safe anchorage in Bantry Bay where repairs could be carried out. The task was made all the more difficult by some of the worst storms in living memory.

On September 6th 1991, another important change occurred when the move of the company's headquarters took place from Hatch Street to new premises at Beech Hill Office Campus at Clonskeagh. The company had been located in the Hatch Street premises for some 21 years and the move to Clonskeagh was prompted by the expiry of the lease at Hatch Street, which was owned by the Irish Airline Pilots Pension Fund. A major advantage of the new premises was that they had been designed for the latest technology. Voice, data and power cables were placed under floors and above the suspended ceilings so that it was possible to locate a computer, telephone or desk anywhere in the building – something which had not been possible in the older Hatch Street building. Following the move to Beech Hill, an Open Day was held when a blessing was invoked on the new Shell House, its staff and their families by Monsignor Dick Sherry and Canon Dick Bertram.

Another important opening was the order of the day at Cork when guests, including the Lord Mayor of Cork, sailed from Custom House Quay to Tivoli on the mv *Cill Airne* where Desmond O'Malley TD, Minister for Industry and Commerce, formally opened 'Cork Bulk Storage Limited' – Shell Chemical Ireland's bulk liquid storage terminal at Tivoli Industrial Estate. This new facility was the first purpose-built sea-fed chemicals storage terminal in the Cork region and the facility allowed storage of bulk liquids

Patrick Lynch

Appointed Managing Director of Irish Shell in May 1990, Pat Lynch, who had joined the Shell Group as Managing Director of the Colas Group of companies in Ireland in 1982 and who since 1985 had held appointments with Shell International Petroleum Company and with Shell (UK) in London.

which form key raw materials for the chemical and pharmaceutical manufacturing industry in Ireland. Interestingly, at an increasingly environmentally aware time, the new facility, by substituting sea freight from Europe for road tanker delivery gave the added positive benefit of reducing tanker mileage on Irish roads by around a quarter of a million miles per annum.

The same month, November 1991, also brought tragedy at sea when two cargo ships, the mv *Kilkenny* and the mv *Hasselwerder*, collided near the entrance to Dublin Port. The *Kilkenny*, a B+I Line vessel, sustained serious damage which resulted in it sinking and the loss of three crewmen. Two containers bound for Shell Chemicals – one containing SAP 9423, a Class Three product used as an additive for Shell Unleaded petrol, and the other 20 tonnes of non-hazardous plastic, were found to be unaccounted for from the *Kilkenny's* cargo and Irish Shell's emergency procedures were swiftly put into action. The container holding SAP 9423 was subsequently located afloat in the bay and was recovered and towed to port, where under the supervision of Irish Shell personnel, it was removed from the water. The second container with the non-hazardous plastic proved more elusive and was never recovered.

In the Spring of 1992, in another significant and far-reaching development, Irish Shell announced its intention of introducing a new shop concept to the Irish market. The purpose of the initiative was to introduce a distinctive brand and style to shops on Irish Shell retail sites. This was a radical departure from past practice and signalled the company's growing awareness of the increasing significance of 'convenience' shops on Irish petrol forecourts. However, despite the spring announcement, it was not until the autumn that the first of what would grow into an extensive chain of convenience stores was opened at Fairies Cross, Tralee. The new stores were titled 'Select' and over the following years as the network expanded, brought a strong, new brand image to Shell forecourts across the country.

Another notable landmark occurred in March of the following year, when the new Irish Shell terminal at Cork was officially re-opened by the Minister of State for Energy, Noel Treacy TD. Managing Director Patrick Lynch reiterated Irish Shell's confidence in the future growth of business in the Munster region which had *"already been demonstrated by the opening of Shell Chemicals bulk storage facility at Tivoli in 1991 and the investment in the Irish Shell terminal of over £4m. representing the company's commitment to its business in the area."* The investment in Cork was part of a £50m. improvement programme by Irish Shell over the ten years leading up to

Cork Terminal Re-Opening 1993

On Wednesday March 10th 1993, the new Irish Shell terminal at Cork was officially opened. The most environmentally advanced oil distribution centre in the region, the new terminal represented a major part of Irish Shell's £4m. investment in the Cork area. Pictured clockwise from top left: Two general views of the new tanker loading gantrys; The new bottom-loading gantry in operation with Philip Murphy, Terminal Manager and Michael Hayes; Sean Curtin, Managing Director of South of Ireland Petroleum.

1993, in the continuing re-development and upgrading of its facilities countrywide. Through this, Irish Shell could claim to support the direct employment of nearly 1,000 people, either directly in the company, in its subsidiaries or through its Authorised Distributor network.

The introduction of a written Environmental Policy in July 1993 saw Irish Shell take a major step forward amongst Irish companies with regard to its treatment of the environment. The Environmental Policy had been developed to help guide staff in their response to the increasing environmental needs of the company, recognising that changes in practices and in facilities might be required should these needs not be met. As a result, in the development of its business, products and services, the company is now guided by overall environmental impact criteria. In several areas – most notably in the introduction of Unleaded fuels to the Irish market, when it was the first company to market Unleaded 95 octane petrol on a national basis – Irish Shell has given a pioneering lead.

And, in another change which served to point the way to other developments in the future, Shell Chemicals Ireland took over responsibility for marketing group petrochemical products in Northern Ireland from Shell Chemical UK.

The company broke new ground with the April 1993 launch of a free forecourt magazine entitled *Shell People*. A totally new concept in forecourt retailing, *Shell People* was produced to a very high standard and gave Irish Shell a powerful new marketing and communications tool. *Shell People* would continue to be successfully published for the next four years.

One of the many events featured in the pages of *Shell People* was the Shell Air Spectacular of 1993 held at the Air Corp's Casement Aerodrome base where 70,000 people thrilled to the aerobatics skills of the Alfajet pilots of *Patrouille de France*, the famous French national display team. The Shell sponsorship continued a connection with public air displays which stretched back to the very start of Irish aviation and the first aviation meeting held at Leopardstown in 1910. Other stars of the Spectacular were the Swedish Air Force Drakens, particularly memorable for the amount of noise they generated, and the French Air Force Mirage 2000 fighter jets.

Another event featured in the pages of *Shell People,* was the Shell Dream Ticket promotion which saw no less than 420 winners attend the Irish matches in USA World Cup '94 at New York and Orlando as guests of Irish Shell. Needless to say, a wonderful time was had by all and the trip soon earned its place in Irish Shell mythology!

World Beaters

Bob Kievits, Retail Manager, and Gerry McManus, Marketing Manager, had key roles in Irish Shell during the difficult period at the end of the 1980s and early 1990s.
And the cards?
Together, both men were winners of the 1990 Shell World-wide Bridge Tournament. Their score of 71.7 per cent was the highest returned by any players in Shell companies from all over the world. The runner-up was France with the Netherlands in third place.

Booked!

Matt Langan of Irish Shell looks quite happy to be 'booked' by Superintendent Ray Campion while Jimmy Cope, Chairman of the Road Safety Committee, looks on. The occasion was the 1990 St. Patrick's Day Parade in Dublin's O'Connell Street. The 'car' is one of a fleet sponsored by Irish Shell at the Children's Road Safety School at Clontarf run by Dublin Corporation and with which the company has been involved since its inception.

A major high profile business coup was achieved when the mv *Veronica* – the biggest fishing trawler operating in Europe and the biggest one-person owned fishing trawler in the world – contracted to be fuelled and lubricated by Irish Shell through Donegal Oil Company. The mv *Veronica* cost £25m. and was owned by Kevin McHugh of Killybegs. Subsequently, following a fire while the mv *Veronicia* was in Harland & Wolff's Belfast shipyard, she was replaced by an even larger vessel, the mv *Atlantic Dawn*.

A link back to the earliest days of the company was broken in September 1995, when Irish Shell changed its advertising agency from the McConnell Group to Bell Advertising, part of the Ogilvy & Mather Group who handled Shell business in many countries throughout the world. The appointment was to be relatively short-lived as the account switched to DDFH&B in September 1997. This was as a result of the appointment of the J Walter Thompson Group – of which DDFH&B is part – as the advertising agency for Shell across Europe.

At around the same time, Irish Shell became involved in two major controversies, which, while not of its own making, served to demonstrate that the company must now take not just a global as well as a local view, but also an element of responsibility for the actions of Shell operating companies in other locations. The first of these affairs was in relation to the deep-sea disposal of the Brent Spar offshore storage and loading facility. In April 1995, Greenpeace activists, accompanied by some media representatives, had boarded the Brent Spar with the intention of preventing Shell from carrying out its deep-sea disposal. At first, this action received relatively little media coverage, but, following the Annual General Meeting in London of the Shell Transport and Trading Company, media interest increased substantially amongst politicians, the public and environmentalists. As a result of intense public interest in Britain and elsewhere, Shell UK reversed its original decision and made a commitment *"to abandon deep-water disposal and seek from the UK authorities a licence for onshore disposal."*

The interest shown by various parties here necessitated Irish Shell providing the key facts of the case to allow informed discussion take place on the complex issues involved. The decision to abandon the deep-sea disposal of Brent Spar took the heat out of the debate in Ireland. However, if the Brent Spar disposal raised complex issues, it served only as a curtain raiser for the next controversy to effect Irish Shell. On this occasion, Irish Shell was drawn into the front-line as it was subjected to adverse media comment, a sit-in at its Head Office and demonstrations at retail sites in Dublin and Galway. In addition, in an unprecedented development, many

The Brent Spar Controversy

The proposed deep-sea disposal of the Brent Spar offshore storage and loading facility, at a site 150 miles off the west coast of Ireland, provoked considerable controversy amongst the Irish public and politicians in 1995. As a result of intense public interest, Shell UK reversed its decision and sought a licence for on-shore disposal.

customers wrote to Irish Shell expressing their disapproval of Shell's role in the issue.

The controversy involved was, of course, that pertaining to events in Nigeria relating to the Ogoni people, their Movement for Survival of the Ogoni People (MOSOP) and the campaign against Shell's presence and operations in their country. This campaign was intensified following the execution of the MOSOP leader, Mr Ken Saro Wiwa, and eight others by the Nigerian authorities. As a result of the intense interest shown in the issue in Ireland by politicians and the public alike, Managing Director Patrick Lynch and Public Affairs Manager Declan Fallon travelled to Nigeria and spent a week with the Shell Petroleum Development Company learning at first hand the complex problems involved. Early the following year (1996), as a result of an invitation from the Joint Committee on Foreign Affairs to Irish Shell to give a presentation on Shell's involvement in Nigeria, Emeka Achebe, Director of Environmental Affairs and Human Resources with the Shell Petroleum Company of Nigeria, travelled to Dublin. The visit took place just ten days after the request was first made and Emeka Achebe's measured and unemotional account of the factual involvement and contribution made by Shell in the Niger Delta region was particularly impressive. Widespread media interest in the visit also resulted in appearances on 'The Pat Kenny Show' and on 'Marketplace'. Perhaps the result of this intense scrutiny of Shell's Nigerian operation is best summarised by the final part of Patrick Lynch's report on his fact-finding visit to the region:

> *I am fully satisfied that Shell, as a minority partner in SPDC, albeit being the operator, is acting in a responsible and professional manner, taking great pains to ensure that its relations with the communities in whose territory it operates, were as good as possible and that it responded in some measure to the most basic needs of those communities, always bearing in mind that it is not Government and should not be substitute for the proper responsibilities of Government in those areas. I am also satisfied that the extreme accusations levelled at Shell are without basis or foundation, and that they are exaggerated to attain political objectives which is contrary to the way Shell companies are allowed to operate.*

A major announcement at the start of 1996, saw Shell International renew its backing for the Ferrari Formula One team and its drivers, the German Michael Schumacher and Irishman Eddie Irvine. This was a return to a successful partnership which had existed when Shell previously raced in

The Ogoni Issue – 1996

The controversy surrounding the plight of the Ogoni People in Nigeria led to Managing Director Pat Lynch and Public Affairs Manager Declan Fallon, making a week-long visit to Nigeria in 1996 to learn at first-hand about the complex problems involved. Declan Fallon is seen in the top photograph preparing for one of the many flights made by the duo within Nigeria.

Just ten days after a request from the Joint Committee on Foreign Affairs to Irish Shell to give a presentation on Shell's involvement in Nigeria, Emeka Achebe, Director of Environmental Affairs with the Shell Company in Nigeria, travelled to Dublin and impressed all with his factual and unemotional presentation of the facts.

Formula 1 with Ferrari from 1951 to 1973. The cost of the partnership had, however, dramatically increased and carried a price-tag of $25 million. Nevertheless, it was money the company regarded as well-spent and was to give rise to considerable success in the following years, both on the track and in the marketing arena. For Irish Shell, the inclusion of Northern Ireland driver, Eddie Irvine, in the team's line-up was a significant bonus. The association between Shell and Ferrari continues successfully to this day, and no other oil company can match Shell's success in Formula 1, a total of no less than 20 Drivers and 14 Constructors titles having been won using Shell products.

Irish Shell has long had particularly close links with the Air Corps and their celebration in 1996 of 75 years of military aviation support and service to the State with an Air Display at their Casement Aerodrome base, was an event with which the company was especially pleased to be associated as the major patron. Representatives of many of the world's air forces were present, and an outstanding two days flying took place in a uniquely friendly, yet efficient atmosphere. No doubt many younger spectators left Casement with the sound of jet engines reverberating in their heads and a desire to follow in the footsteps of the pilots they had witnessed.

There was change at the top of Shell on October 1st 1996, when Michael Forde took over the reins as Managing Director. An accountant by profession, Michael joined Irish Shell as Treasurer/Company Secretary in 1984 and having spent three years with Shell in London in Trading and Chemicals, he returned to Irish Shell in 1989 as Finance Director and in 1995 became Marketing Director.

An early event during Michael Forde's time as Managing Director was the return to Ireland of the Shell Wonderful World of Golf when, in July 1997, Mount Juliet hosted a match between Tom Watson and Fred Couples. The referee was none other than the famous Irish amateur golfer, Joe Carr, who had himself played in one of the Shell Wonderful World of Golf matches back in 1965 when he played Al Geiberger at Killarney.

Perhaps the most significant development for the long-term to happen under Michael Forde's leadership has been the coming together of the Shell operations in Northern Ireland and the Republic. The occasion was marked by a dinner held in Jury's Hotel, Dublin on November 1st 1997 when over 80% of the combined staff of Shell and their partners were in attendance.

Up until then, Shell in Ireland was run on the basis of the geographic separation of North and South, but in recent years Shell's business has been breaking down geographic borders with developments on both the

Michael Forde

On October 1st 1996, Michael Forde was appointed Managing Director and Country Chairman. An accountant by profession, Michael joined Irish Shell as Treasurer/Company Secretary in 1984 and having spent three years with Shell in London in Trading and Chemicals, he returned to Irish Shell in 1989 as Finance Director and in 1995 became Marketing Director.

European and global levels. Similarly, many major Irish companies were moving to conduct their business on an all-Ireland basis. It was only a matter of time before that new spirit impacted on Irish Shell and after several false starts during the preceding five years, a study team was set up early in 1997 to solve the problem. Comprising Paul Barrington, Frank Bergin, Alwyn Hoy and Colin Nisbett, their task was to come up with an 'Island of Ireland' implementation plan. Starting in January 1997, the team met almost every two weeks, alternating between Dublin and Belfast, their report was presented to management in Shell UK and Irish Shell in April and endorsed. There then followed a period of discussion with the various parties in Shell Northern Ireland, Shell UK and Irish Shell, covering the implications for all concerned in implementing the plan, which saw full integration achieved from January 1st 1998.

Two other significant challenges during Michael Forde's reign were the repercussions from the Brent Spar and Ogoni controversies. These had brought the issue of Shell's corporate reputation to centre stage. Shell's response was to engage in a long and deep process of consultation with a number of external parties with a view to fully understanding the change in society's expectations which had undoubtedly occurred regarding how a multinational oil company should behave. This lead to the publication of a series of annual Shell reports, commencing in 1999 with 'Profits and Principles – does there have to be a choice?' As Irish Shell had been significantly impacted, particularly by the Ogoni issue, a similar process of external consultation was undertaken in Ireland through a Stakeholder Forum, attended by representatives of NGO's and other interested parties as well as company staff.

And in line with its increased emphasis on the Environment, Shell introduced a new petrol, Shell Pura, across its network in 1998. Shell Pura, which has been an important and successful new product for Shell is an ultra-clean petrol, specially formulated for customers who want the cleanest petrol available to help cut traffic pollution.

The all-Ireland theme was again evident with the awarding of the Nobel Prize for Peace jointly to John Hume and David Trimble in 1999 for their efforts to secure peace in Northern Ireland. The occasion was marked by Irish Shell hosting a reception and dinner for the prize winners and their families and friends in Oslo following the Awards ceremony.

From its earliest days, Irish Shell has been recognised as a good employer. Wages and conditions were amongst the best in the country and these are backed by a pension scheme which even today has few rivals in

Shell in the Island of Ireland

On January 1st 1998, Shell on the Island of Ireland came together to run their business on an all-Ireland basis. 'Shell on the Island of Ireland', as the initiative was named, was the result of almost a years hard work by an implementation team and occurred after several false starts over the preceding five years. The event was celebrated at a Dinner held on November 1st 1997 at Jury's Hotel, Dublin ,which was attended by over 80% of the staff of Shell and their partners. Our photograph shows (from left): Declan Fallon, Public Affairs Manager of Irish Shell; Margaret and Liam O'Kane, Managing Director of Shell Northern Ireland – and Michael Forde, Managing Director of Irish Shell and Country Chairman.

An Historic Day is Oslo

On the occasion of the awarding of the Nobel Prize for Peace jointly to John Hume and David Trimble in 1999 for their efforts to secure peace in Northern Ireland, Irish Shell hosted a reception and dinner for the prize winners and their families and friends in Oslo following the Awards ceremony. The top photograph shows (from left): Liam O'Kane, Managing Director of Shell Northern Ireland; John and Pat Hume; Declan Fallon, Public Affairs Manager of Irish Shell.

209

Ireland or further afield. Contact with pensioners is maintained through the Pensioners Liaison Representative, a role today fulfilled by Jack Dunne, who visits retired staff in their homes. Upon the death of a fund member assistance is given to the family with pension, social welfare and income tax applications. At other times, the Pension Liaison Representative visit consists of a chat about old times and a welcome update on how old colleagues are faring.

Following a short illness, another link with the past was lost when Bernard Nolan died peacefully at the end of 1999 aged 77. In a short tribute in *Eolas* Magazine, Noel Tierney wrote:

> *Bernard Nolan brought to bear on whatever he did a keen, meticulous and uncompromising intelligence and a fixity of purpose. He could make a 'nourishing nibble' of anyone who did not do their job efficiently. He had a short fuse for dealing with nerds, cant and especially prevarication: whether the latter came from bureaucrats or even Government Ministers.*
>
> *But he commanded the confident goodwill and respect of all who came to engage openly with him. He kept people at arm's length, and yet felt strongly about them. If a colleague were to find themselves in a jam, or in some straits, they could count on attentive help and understanding.*

The Society of the Irish Motor Industry, with whom the Oil Industry has had difficult relations at times in the past, honoured Michael Forde by appointing him President of the Society in June 2000. Also in 2000, Professor Mary Lambkin, became the first woman to be appointed to the Board of Shell Ireland. A former Chairman of the Marketing Society, Professor Lambkin was the Dean of Postgraduate Studies at the Michael Smurfit Graduate School of Business at University College, Dublin.

On October 31st 2001, Michael Forde retired and was replaced as Country Chairman by John McDonagh. John is a graduate of both UCD and the Marketing Institute. He joined Irish Shell in October 1981 and has held positions in Supply and Distribution, Petrochemicals and most recently in Retail.

Irish Shell has endured, in its many manifestations, through times of profound change for this country as well as for the company and its employees. Great challenges have been faced and overcome and in so doing, a new purpose and drive is abroad. So too, is a new confidence that Irish Shell will remain at the forefront of change within the Irish energy industry and will ably meet the challenges of the new century – just as its men and

John McDonagh

On October 31st 2001, Michael Forde retired and was replaced as Country Chairman by John McDonagh. John is a graduate of both UCD and the Marketing Institute. He joined Irish Shell in October 1981 and has held positions in Supply and Distribution, Petrochemicals and most recently in Retail.

women have been doing successfully throughout Shell's first century in Ireland.

Shell Voices

The Trials of the Tribulus

I got the word on a Sunday that the ship was in trouble and flew to Cork with John Withrington and then on to Bantry where we joined up with the team from Shell Marine Tankers who had arrived from the UK. We waited through the night as the ship battled through high seas making its way to the safe haven of Bantry Bay. She had lost four plates below the waterline, they had peeled like a sardine can, and afterwards we discovered the hole was big enough to put two double decker buses through. It was with some trepidation that we rose before dawn on the Monday morning and flew by helicopter down the bay to meet the ship coming in.

My first memory of the ship itself was of this huge tanker coming up the bay, listing heavily with her 130,000 tonnes of ore on board and being escorted by trawlers with a 'U' shaped boom to contain the leaking bunker oil. When she reached safe anchorage, we landed on one of the holds so that the damage could be inspected. This was my first time in a helicopter and I can still remember the pilot trying to put the chopper down on a heaving, slanting deck. He waited for the deck to rise and as he tried to land the deck went away from him and as he went after it, it started to come back up at him – my heart was in my mouth but his skill got us down safely.

The Shell team were so professional, they were on site for three months and took over entirely the Westlodge Hotel where the crisis centre was based. Specialists of all descriptions were brought in; mariners, marine engineers, environmental specialists, marine biologists, public affairs and legal. Temporary repairs were carried out on the ship in the bay, below water the hole was plugged, claims for compensation were handled on site and settled locally in the Hotel, the clean-up was managed with regard to the wishes of the local community.

Declan Fallon – Corporate Services Manager

Painful Times

When Jim (Beveridge) came in 1982 there were 550 people in the company, when he left there were 330 and when I left there were 140, so these were dramatic and painful times. We were internally focused trying to restructure our costs. What Albert Reynolds did was to accelerate an inevitable process for the oil companies, who had to restructure their business in Ireland if they were to survive.

John Withrington – Managing Director 1986-1990

"...the best possible spirit"

All of the restructuring that was done was completed without any "blood on the floor"- having been started by Jim Beveridge, continued by John Withrington and then I had the

212

'LiveWIRE'

An international programme developed by Shell and originally started in Scotland in 1983, Shell LiveWIRE was launched in Ireland in April 1999 by Noel Tracey TD, Minister for Science, Technology and Commerce. Developed by Shell to encourage young people to become interested in setting up in business and in working for themselves, by the start of 2002 over 360,000 young people world-wide have benefited from the LiveWIRE programme. LiveWIRE provides practical advice on setting up a business in Ireland, provides management training for start-up businesses and runs the annual Young Business Start-Up Awards. The photograph shows Michael Forde and Minister for Science, Technology and Commerce Noel Tracey TD with Celtel Limited, Galway - winners of the 2000 Young Business Start-Up Award.

relatively easy task of completing it. The hardest bullet was bitten by John Withrington who decided that they had to go again. It was blood-less, it was done in the best possible spirit and it saved the business, and of course, we led the way in the Shell Group in that level of restructuring and contracting out so much of our activity.

Patrick Lynch – Managing Director, 1990-1996

A Focused Man

Gerry McManus was renowned for his ability to focus on business as the late Jim Kennedy, no mean driver himself, found out.

Gerry had expressed a desire to be driven at rally speeds over a special stage of the Donegal Rally. I arranged to act as a 'Sweeper' car running ahead of the rally competitors and behind the Official cars. As we waited to start Gerry and I were discussing a business issue. We strapped ourselves in and set off after the Official cars. Gerry continued the discussion but I was far too busy to listen and was finding myself put to the pin of my collar to keep up with the other cars. We just about did keep up – despite several 'moments' – and eventually reached the end of the special stage. All the while, Gerry had continued talking about business as if nothing untoward was happening and got out of the car without pausing in his line of thought or mentioning the close shaves we'd just had. Now that's what I call a focused man...

Jim Kennedy, Donegal Oil Company

The Next Time!

One elderly lady, a widow of a Shell pensioner, turned 100, and she lived down in County Clare in a nursing home. I arranged for flowers and a card to be sent to her with our best wishes and congratulations. As it happened, soon afterwards, my wife Mary and I were in the area and decided to go and say hello to this wonderful lady. So having arrived at the nursing home, we met the matron who told us she had had a very busy day and was probably a little tired. Additionally, she was a little hard of hearing. "Mary', the matron said, "This is Mr lynch and his wife, the man that sent you the flowers, the managing director of Irish Shell". "Oh", she says, "How are you?" And I said, "How are you?" "Do you know what", she says, "The next time send me chocolates, I can't see the fecking flowers!"

Patrick Lynch – Managing Director, 1990-1996

Infuriatingly Himself...

He was infuriatingly himself,
Not always right but never wrong,
An expert in dry humour,
In logic very strong.

Extract from the Memorial card issued by his family on the occasion of Bernard Nolan's death in 1999

The Shell Donegal Rally

The Donegal International Rally, with support from Irish Shell, the Donegal Oil Company and the Inishowen Oil Company has grown down the years to become one of the most popular and successful motorsport events in Ireland. In a sponsorship which spans more than 20 years, there have been many great moments but few drivers names are so closely associated with the event as that of the late Bertie Fisher, seen here (top photograph) competing in the 1992 event in a Subaru. Below is a group with the 1998 winner. They are (from left): Sean Kelly; (MD Inishowen Oil), James O'Shea (co-driver); Kelly Anne Fleming; Andrew Nesbitt (driver); Michael Forde – Managing Director, Irish Shell and Brian Rowan, (MD Donegal Oil).

Its more than making Money

The people who really impressed me while we were going through all the difficulties of running Irish Shell were our Authorised Distributors and I remember thinking at that time, what a great strength they were to the company and how valuable were these local connections. I think particularly in the peninsulas – I'm thinking of the Kellys in Inishowen and the Blennerhassetts in Kerry – there the loyalty was fierce. They have a passion to retain the business. It's more than making money, they were proud to be associated with Shell and it made me feel good at a time when the rest of the company was struggling. I think that helped bring us through a very difficult period.

John Withrington – Managing Director 1986-1990

Oh Mammy!

The next morning another plane was despatched to pick us up at Warri and as our small jet thundered down the runway for take-off, we had a bird strike followed by a bang and a screech of brakes. My first thought was "How long is this runway?" My second thought was "Do I accept a transfusion in this country?" My third thought was "We're still on this runway?" My fourth thought was "I'll take anybody's blood if this plane will ever stop!" My fifth thought was "Oh Mammy". Eventually the plane stopped and returned to the terminal.

Declan Fallon, Corporate Services Manager, tells of his experiences during a fact-finding visit to Nigeria.

The Shell Wonderful World of Golf

When it came to our attention that matches were once more being played, we set about seeking a match for Ireland. Michael Forde and I went to Scotland to meet Terry Jastrow, the producer from Jack Nicklaus Productions who were making the film, to discuss an Irish match. The discussion got around to who should play and in our company at the time was Fred Couples who had played Greg Norman that day. He told us that he had never played competitively in Ireland and would love the chance. Immediately, Michael picked up on this and extended an invitation to play at Mount Juliet. Freddie was delighted to accept. The second player more or less selected himself. Tom Watson at this stage was a regular visitor to Ballybunion prior to every British open, and was loved by the Irish golf fans. An invitation was extended and he readily accepted.

Declan Fallon – Corporate Services Manager

75 Years without Problems...

Before the coming together of Shell operations North and South – about 1996 – McMullans were trying to arrange supplies for their Northern Ireland operation from Shell UK. In frustration out of the difficulties he was experiencing in the negotiations, Noel McMullan produced an invoice from Irish Shell, dated 1922, complete with 2d stamp as receipt, and declared "in dealing with Irish Shell over 75 years we never had problems like this in our negotiations"!

Teresa Cosgrave, Supply Manager.

Irish Shell's Authorised Distributors

Irish Shell's Authorised Distributors were pictured together on the occasion of Michael Forde's retirement in November 2001. Back row (left to right): Declan Fallon, Irish Shell; Arthur McMahon, Donegal Oil; Declan Carmody, Capital Oil; Sean Whelan, Vale Oil; Kevin Keyes, Glen Fuel Services; Roland Blennerhassett, Kerry Petroleum; Michael Keane, Shannonside Oil; Eugene Dalton, Corrib Oil; Frank Bergin, Irish Shell.
Front row (left to right): Sean Curtin, South of Ireland Petroleum; Triana Rankin, Vale Oil; Michael Forde; Seamus Kelly, Inishowen Oil; Nicholas Nolan, Leinster Petroleum; Sean Kelly, Inishowen Oil.

I had a happy life in Shell

Shell in my years was not paternalistic but the closest thing to it. I do believe it was particularly well regarded in the industry. Good staff motivation was prompted by the diligent application of two useful human resource aids which helped to create an environmentally satisfactory workplace. First, the annual staff appraisal system which in turn facilitated the second – the concept of endeavouring, where practicable, to arrange the transfer, by way of promotion or lateral move, staff members after five or ten years in the job. I had a happy life in Shell

Paddy Foley – Retail Services Manager

Sporting Moments

The 2001 Shell Johnny Mathis Golf Classic held at The Royal Belfast Golf Club to raise funds for NSPCC programmes in Northern Ireland. Pictured presenting the cheque for £40,000 to Pamela Scott (NSPCC) are Michael Forde, Chairman of Shell in Ireland and singing legend Johnny Mathis. In the second photograph, Charlie Swan rides Istabraq, trained by Aidan O'Brien, to a famous victory in the Shell Champion Hurdle in 1999.

Appendix 1

The Golden Age of Shell Advertising

1924 HM Bateman

From the days of its earliest advertisements, Shell has sold not simply products, but rather the brand 'Shell'. From the mid-1920s and on through the 1930s this proposition was expressed in advertising, almost entirely through the mediums of posters and press, in a series of advertisements that was to win for this period the description 'The Golden Age of Shell Advertising'.

Although the greatest part of the credit for this era must go to Jack Beddington, Shell's UK Advertising Manager from 1932 to 1939, in truth, the sell-assured style of Shell, the omnipotent world brand, was beginning to take shape even earlier. By the beginning of the 1920s Shell poster advertising in particular, using the poster panels on the side of its delivery lorries and tankers, had begun to display a self assuredness that pointed the way to what would be achieved in the 1930s.

Most of the Shell advertising that was used in Ireland in the Free State of the time, originated in the UK, but there were important exceptions with advertisements also being produced locally for Irish Shell by McConnell's Advertising Service in Dublin. Because of its importance as the visible manifestation of the company to so many people, what follows is a selection of the advertisements produced during this period and which appeared in Ireland when the Brand stance taken for Shell, helped shape so much of its future.

Some of Shell's earliest advertising concerns the company's achievements in various events, be they pioneering aviation flights or motor sporting successes. Press advertisements used in Ireland to advertise Shell's involvement with the Dublin to Belfast Air Race of 1912 and the conquest of the Atlantic by Alcock and Brown are portrayed elsewhere in this book. The advertisement from 1923 which follows combined the Atlantic flight with flights to Australia and Africa in an imaginative and highly stylised treatment which must have had a strong impact through its originality.

222

Carbon and its build-up on engine parts was blamed for many of the ills of early motorists. Fuels which reduced or prevented its build-up were advertised by several companies in the early days of motoring and Shell was no exception. In this 1927 press advertisement, the dreaded Carbon is given form and banished by the 'Anti-Carbon Pair – Shell Motor Oil and Petrol'.

For an
Improved Wayside

IN the early days of motoring, garages were comparatively few and far between and they needed signs to indicate to motorists where their essential requirements could be secured.

With the increase in the number of garages, however, the number and variety of enamelled iron signs have multiplied and they now constitute a serious defacement of the wayside.

The justification for these signs has finally become nullified by the present-day general adoption of petrol pumps and oil cabinets—essential items in modern service to motorists.

In view of these facts Shell-Mex (Dublin) Limited wish to announce a policy of

NO SHELL SIGNS

Hereafter no new Shell signs will be issued, except essential designations of brand, grade, price, etc., upon petrol pumps and lubricating oil cabinets.

Also, we shall urge all retailers to allow us to remove and destroy all other existing exterior advertisements of our products.

Shell-Mex (Dublin) Ltd.

Many of Shell's early advertisements addressed the motorist's concerns, as in the case of the 'Banish Carbon' advertisement. A famous court case taken by the company against a motor spirit retailer who was selling other inferior brands as Shell resulted in this widespread practice being given considerable publicity. Shell followed its legal success with a series of advertisements reinforcing the authenticity of the product sold from its kerbside petrol pumps, an example of which follows.

The ending of the First World War had the effect of creating many hundreds of thousands of potential new motorists, who having sampled motorised transport during the conflict, no longer regarded it as the preserve of the rich and titled. The impetus that this brought to bear on the motor industry to produce smaller, cheaper-to-run motor cars bore fruit over the next few years. As a result, car ownership became possible for many who had previously been excluded. The resultant freedom to explore the countryside was a popular theme for car advertising of the time, and is the basis of this 1923 advertisement titled 'Carried Unanimously'.

For a period following the launch of its range of motor lubricating oils in the early 1920s, Shell Oils and Shell Motor Spirit were advertised together in press and poster advertisements. Both are ingeniously woven into the strikingly assured illustration of this 1922 example, "On the Right Road – Every Drop Tells".

SHELL MOTOR LUBRICATING **OILS**
"Every Drop Tells"
SHELL MOTOR **SPIRIT**
Shell-Mex, Ltd.
DUBLIN OFFICE—70 Grafton Street.

To my mind, although Shell advertising had been demonstrating a growing assuredness in the early 1920s, it was with the series of Jim Bateman advertisements – press and poster – that Shell advertising began to come of age. Simple themes, brilliantly executed, they have an impact achieved by few advertisements of the time. Whether in black and white in the pages of The Motor News magazine or on the poster boards on the sides of Shell lorries and tankers, the Bateman series is a joy to behold.

In 1925 a striking series of posters was commissioned from the artist John Roland Barker for use on lorry poster boards. Their common theme of SEE IRELAND FIRST and attractive illustrations using flat colour is particularly strong. I suspect that initially, there were four featuring

The Jim Bateman Posters

JUBILATION

DETERMINATION

DISCRIMINATION

APPRECIATION

RECOMMENDATION

EXASPERATION

APPRECIATION

SALVATION

See Ireland First

Glendalough, County Wicklow

Devil's Isle, Killarney

Blackrock Castle, Cork

Ballynahinch, Connemara

– on Shell (1925)

Dunluce Castle, Ulster

Giant's Causeway, Ulster

Happy Valley, Ulster

Lough Erne, Ulster

Glendalough, County Wicklow; Blackrock Castle, Cork; Devil's Island, Killarney and Ballinahinch, Connemara. It would appear that a second set featuring Ulster subjects followed and these – distinguishable by the word ULSTER in large lettering on the name scroll – included the following subjects: Dunluce Castle; The Giant's Causeway; Lough Erne and Happy Valley. Today, they remain very striking with perhaps the Devil's Island and Glendalough posters being the most visually arresting.

Success advertising continued throughout this period and two good examples are the advertisements for the 1930 Irish International Grand Prix and the 1931 Tourist Trophy Races.

The introduction of Quick starting Shell in 1930 led to a small series of advertisements which appeared in the Irish national daily newspapers. Simple and strong in execution, this example conveys the self-depreciating humour that has characterised Shell advertising down through the years.

Recalling the SEE IRELAND FIRST posters of 1925, an apparently one-off poster was produced in 1932 featuring Castle Howard, County Wicklow. The artist was George Bissill (1896-1973) who was a landscape painter and who also designed furniture and for a time, worked as a pavement artist.

A final poster featuring an Irish landscape was commissioned in 1939 from the artist Eve Kirk. Eve Kirk was a painter born in the early 1900s who spent a considerable time in Greece and the Dalmatian Islands, making wonderful paintings of the mountain villages and towns and the brilliant Mediterranean light. Her work has always sought to integrate man and the environment he has created for himself. It is this understanding of light that

she has brought to this unusual view of the River Liffey which flows through Dublin. Above all else, the painting seems to say that here, there is time to linger, to think, to look around.

Although, the Golden Age of Shell advertising passed with the ending of the 1930s, Lorry posters continued to be used up into the mid-1950s, new posters going up on these mobile display panels each month.

Appendix 2

The Shell Trophies

The BURNS CUP
Presented by J. A. Burns in 1926

1926	D Browne	1936	J A Halpin.	1957	T F O'Loughlin
1927	D L Ryan	1937	M J Murphy.	1958	D J Garvey
1928	H G Blee	1938	E C Bourke.	1959	P Prendergast
1929	D L Ryan	1939	J F Dixon	1960	P Creagh
1930	W T Telford	1940	H C Blee	1961	P B Bellew
1931	D L Ryan	1952	T H Marchment	1962	P Delaney
1932	D Persee Joynt.	1953	P J Anthony	1963	F G McArdle
1933	Eileen Cleary	1954	B M O'Reilly	1964	R Lonergan
1934	M E Morrow	1955	B P O'Neill	1965	J C Farrell
1935	J O'Doherty	1956	N G F O'Connell	1966	R Lonergan

1967	M Foley	1985	J Condon	1996	C G Rowden
1980	R Lonergan	1986	C G Rowden	1997	M Coghlan
1981	A W D Smith	1987	P J Crerar	1998	J Downing
1982	G Stone	1988	P J Crerar	1999	Not won
1983	E Lynch	1989	P Keogh	2000	R Acton
1984	E Lynch	1995	I Mackey	2001	T Dolphin

The JOYCE ROSE BOWL
Presented by Walter Joyce in 1982
for Ladies Golf

1982	M Dalton
1983	M Kerwick
1984	D Gormley
1985	M Kerwick
1986	P Lennon
1987	G Bradley
1988	G Byrne
1989	P Keogh
1990	I Mackey
1991	S Farrell
1992	G Byrne
1993	P Higgins

Other Trophies

The Irish Shell Tennis Perpetual Challenge Cup for Men

1935	G O'Connor	1961	E W Pigot
1937	G O'Connor	1962	M A Downey
1938	J Weir	1963	D O'Callaghan
1939	J Weir	1964	J P Cosgrave
1948	I W G Horder-	1965	D O'Callaghan
	Despard	1966	D O'Callaghan
1949	K B O'Rourke	1967	R C Feeney
1950	B Franklin	1968-76	K Kelleher
1951	C O'Neill	1977	R Acton
1952	C O'Neill	1978	G Stone
1953	C O'Neill	1979	W Barry
1954	K Wall	1980	W Barrett
1955	K Wall	1981	G Stone
1956	P Berkerrry	1982	W Barrett
1957	C Kiernan	1983	W Barrett
1958	P J Pigot	1984	G Stone
1959	B Gaughran	1985	G Stone
1960	P J Pigot		

The Crawford Young Trophy for Ten Pin Bowling presented by T A Crawford Young in 1964

The Vernon Goodchild Trophy for Match-Play Golf

1984	J Kelly	1991	M Forde
1985	P McCullough	1992	D Fallon
1986	M Kerwick	1993	P Mullins
1987	P McCullough	1994	W Trehy
1988	P J Crerar	1995	T Dolphin
1989	P Lennon	1996	A McGinley
1990	P Keogh	1997	D Fallon

Bibliography

Newspapers and Periodicials

EÓLAS
IRISH SHELL MAGAZINE
MOTORING LIFE
THE IRISH TIMES
THE IRISH INDEPENDENT
THE IRISH PRESS

THE MAGAZINE OF THE SHELL-MEX
  AND BP GROUP
THE MOTOR NEWS
THE SHELLMAN
SIMI MAGAZINE
SHELL BP NEWS
SHELL WORLD INTERNATIONAL

Books

A History of SMBP (1999), 44 Club
The Royal Dutch Petroleum Company 1890–1950, (1950), Shell.
Gray, Tony, *The Lost Years* (1997), Little, Brown & Co.
Howarth, Stephen, *A Century in Oil* (1997), Weidenfeld & Nicholson.
Lane, Andrew, *Austerity Motoring 1939–1950* (1987), Shire.
Litton, Helen, *The World War II Years* (2001), Wolfhound.
Montagu, Lord, McComb, F Wilson, *Behind the Wheel* (1977), Paddington.
Montgomery, Bob, *An Irish Roadside Camera 1896–1906* (1997), Marino.
The Shell Poster Book (1992), Hamish Hamilton.
Murphy, John A, Ireland in the Twentiety Century (1989), Gill & McMillan.
O'Donovan, John, *Wheels and Deals* (1983), Gill & McMillan.
O'Sullivan, R W, An Irishman's Aviation Sketchbook (1988), Irish Aviator.
Oram, Hugh, *The Advertising Book* (1986), MO Books.
Roman, Alan, *The Shell Picture Postcard Book* (1995), Shell UK Limited.

Index

References to photographs appear in bold italics.